The
Quiet
Therapies

Japanese Pathways
to Personal Growth

David K. Reynolds

Afterword by George DeVos

THE UNIVERSITY PRESS OF HAWAII
Honolulu

Library of Congress Cataloging in Publication Data

Reynolds, David K
   The quiet therapies.

   Bibliography: p.
   1. Psychotherapy.   2.   Psychotherapy—Japan.
I.   Title.
RC480.5.R39   616.89'14'0952   80–17611
ISBN 0–8248–0690–5

Contents

Preface

THIS BOOK is about several Japanese psychotherapies. In one way or another, all of them cause the client to spend time isolated, locked up in his own thoughts. I call them the quiet therapies.

During the past ten years, I have been studying these therapies—reading about them; observing them in practice; discussing them with therapists and patients; and, to increase my understanding, undergoing treatment as well as treating others with them.

You may have read about these therapies before—and quite possibly have been misled. The brief articles that have appeared in Western scholarly journals and popular magazines often present a caricature of the philosophy and treatment mode of these therapies that is easy for Western therapists to dismiss. The picture presented is generally one of mystical know-it-alls pushing esoteric practices down the throats of masochistic hero worshipers.

Yet the scores of Japanese practitioners I have interviewed turned out to be neither mystical Oriental exotics nor simpleminded authoritarian traditionalists. They have an educated feel for Western therapies and vast personal experience in treating inquisitive and sensitive clients. Their understanding of human nature is deep and firmly grounded in their practice. They do not always have clearly formulated understandings of why each element of a particular therapeutic procedure works, but they can see the effectiveness and can often accurately predict the course of a patient's cure.

I shall devote a chapter each to describing five therapies: Morita therapy, *naikan*, *seiza*, *shadan*, and Zen. The names are somewhat strange, but when their meaning is understood, some of the haze of mysticism blows away. Morita was the name of the professor of psychiatry who developed the therapy to be discussed in the opening chapter. "Naikan" in Japanese is literally *nai* (inner) and *kan* (observation). Put together they mean "introspection." "Seiza" is *sei* (quiet) and *za* (sitting), an excellent description of this method's primary therapeutic element, as we shall see. "Shadan" means "isolation," and "Zen" is the Japanized pronunciation of the Chinese *Ch'an*, which in turn comes from the Sanskrit *dhyana*, meaning "meditation."

This explanation of the therapies' names serves another purpose, too; in a small way, it represents what I have attempted to do in the book as a whole. If I have accomplished my goal, much of what seems at first strange and Eastern will come to make sense to Western readers. It is important to realize that Japanese psychotherapists don't see their techniques as mystical. Rather, these Eastern therapies represent practical advice and techniques for helping patients deal with typical human problems in living.

In the final chapter we shall look at some of the common themes running through these therapies in order to see if we can learn from them something about the nature of man, the ways our minds work, suffering and joy, and the goals of psychotherapy.

Here and there in the pages that follow, the reader will find information about the effectiveness of these therapies; but the reader should beware of these data. Testing the success of any psychotherapy is a notoriously difficult task. Treatment goals vary; outcomes are hard to measure; control groups are difficult to establish and assess; the elements of some therapeutic procedures cannot be evaluated separately—these are but a few of the difficulties. Results are strongly influenced by such factors as which patients are treated, which ones are asked about the outcome, which ones respond, how the questions are phrased, and what is meant by "cure." Furthermore, even if a patient improves after treatment, it doesn't necessarily mean that the treatment brought about the improvement.

Suffice it to say that the five therapies in this book have a history of clinical success in treating neurosis in Japan and that there are numerous practitioners who find them useful. The goal of this book is not to convince you that these therapies are what you or I or the world needs, but merely to make them understandable. I include the evaluation material to provide some concrete indications that certain people do seem to be helped by the methods of these therapies and that some therapists are attempting to validate their clinical impressions of successful treatment with somewhat more objective numerical data.

Many Japanese therapists have been concerned that westerners write about their methods without ever actually experiencing them. They have a basic distrust of the intellectual mode of knowledge when it is not supported by *taiken* (fundamental body-based experience). My research strategy has been to observe, read about, and discuss these therapies as an outsider; to undergo them as a patient; and to treat others as therapist. By these means the biases of each perspective are somewhat diminished by the others.

I am pleased that my behavioral effort in research, writing and rewriting, discussion, and proofreading have resulted in this book. However, I cannot take credit for the ideas presented here. My thoughts come from "somewhere": they bubble to the surface of my mind. Most often, when I am speaking or writing, I have no precise sense of how a sentence or utterance will end once it has begun. Idea seems to follow idea until somehow I sense an end to the flow or shift to another sequence. If the reader considers his own thinking from this angle, I am certain he will discover that his experience is similar. We are all observers of our own thinking— almost as if we watch ideas flash on the screen of our minds. I do not think in the same sense that I act (i.e., cause my body to move). Thinking occurs. I can take credit only for *writing* the thoughts down, for using the thoughts to provide guidance for effective behavior. These few preceding sentences amplify my belief that this book is a result of my writing but that the ultimate source of the ideas remains unknown. To say such a thing is to be neither modest nor mystical; it is merely to be scrupulously truthful.

Others have contributed information and encouragement. Japanese therapists and scholars, too numerous to mention here, invested their time and skills in my study. My department in the University of Southern California School of Medicine provided the freedom and funding and secretarial support for this writing. Medical students, social workers, and psychiatric residents in my elective seminar on Buddhist-based psychotherapies sharpened my thinking by comparing their experiences and understandings with mine. Claudette Martin, Patti Smith, and Mary Guth patiently

typed and retyped the manuscript. Loving significant others allowed me to isolate myself during this writing, cheerfully taking responsibility for most of the logistics of living. The book must bear
an author's name; the limitations and errors are mine; but, like all
creations, this is a group product.

I
Introduction

THE WESTERN TACTIC of analytic categorization, or breaking things down into either-or categories, presents certain problems when dealing with human beings.

I am not introverted, nor am I extraverted. I am both and neither and combinations of degrees of either at one time, or over a period of time. I am not simply angry when a car cuts in front of me on the freeway. Rather, I feel a mixture of anger and surprise and sorrow and alertness and competitiveness and a mélange of other feelings as well. The Japanese are not merely group oriented. They are among the most self-centered, self-seeking people I have ever encountered. They are also among the most self-sacrificing, unselfish, other-directed peoples of the world. I am not talking here about variations among different Japanese individuals, although tremendous variations do exist; I am talking about variations in one individual over time and situation and even in one individual at one moment.

This multiplicity of meanings, feelings, and thoughts associated with any single act or event will prevent us from ever creating a deterministic science of human behavior across-the-board. If we cannot analyze human events into single categories or even a few categories, then we cannot use these categories as independent variables to explain or predict behavior. Simply stated, when we look within ourselves, we see such complexity from moment to moment that any scientific account of what is going on in us will be simplistic and, to that degree, inaccurate.

Scientists can choose to focus on one aspect of experience or behavior and ignore others—that may help us predict behavior with better-than-chance accuracy—but it is much like trying to illuminate a forest with a flashlight. What is to be done about this presumed impasse? One solution is to recognize the inadequacy of the categorical, formal-analytical mode of thinking and to use it sparingly and for a limited set of problems.

An alternative approach is to use a kind of phenomenological operationalism, something I believe we find in the therapies to be discussed. "Operationalism" means defining something in terms of how one arrives at it. For example, an *operational* definition of a cookie would be something like this: "Take sugar, flour, eggs, water, and so forth; combine them; separate the result into pieces; place on a sheet; bake at a certain temperature—and the result is cookies." In contrast, a *dictionary* definition of a cookie might be something like "a small, round, sweet baked good." The dictionary definition aims at describing *what something is;* the operational definition aims at *how to make or locate it.*

I have argued above that my experiencing of my phenomenal world is very complex. I suspect yours is, too, although of course I can never experience your world directly. So, rather than trying to use dictionarylike categories of experience as science does (that person is "extraverted," "frustrated," "neurotic," "suffering from an Oedipal complex," etc.), an operational approach to human experience suggests: "Do this and this in a situation like this and you will have experience X." For example, the naikan therapist says to his client: "Meditate in this particular way, reflecting about how much others have done for you, how little you have returned to them, and how much trouble you have caused them, and the result will be a mixed experience of guilt and gratitude and a desire to serve your fellow man." When we ask the naikan

therapist why this result occurs, he may give us a long explanation that eventually comes down to "it is human nature to
react in this way to these circumstances." Scientifically,
that's not much of an explanation. But operationally he has
defined a situation that will predictably lead us to a particular set of experiences. That is, he has provided us with a kind
of phenomenological operationalism, a guide to arriving at
certain experiences.

In a scientific experiment we usually control certain conditions and try to predict certain outcomes. The therapists in
this book control certain experiences in their clients. Their
predictions seem to be rather accurate. Their explanations,
thus far, are rather thin and spotty from a scientific perspective. This spottiness will make some people uncomfortable. I
am merely raising the possibility that the fault lies, not in the
lack of ability of these therapists in the field of science, but in
the fundamental orientation of science itself. If limited categorical definitions of human experience are all science can
use, then perhaps no accurate understanding of human experience is possible. But if we allow empathy, introspection,
and operational approaches to experience into respectable
scientific circles, we might begin to map out a fuller predictive science of the mind. If and when that day comes, we will
have much to learn from the practitioners of these "quiet
therapies."

II
Morita Psychotherapy

QUITE NATURALLY, Japanese therapies contain Japanese ways of looking at people and their problems, just as Western therapies contain Western ways of approaching people. Note that I do not claim that these are *the* Japanese views on these topics, because, of course, in Japan, as in the West, one can select from among a variety of perspectives.

The first quiet therapy has a distinctively Japanese flavor. It was concocted in the early 1900s by a philosopher-psychiatrist named Morita Shoma—"concocted" because Morita blended a large measure of Buddhistic thought with the personal accounts of his neurotic patients' problems, added elements of his own experience and thought, borrowed some ideas from Western psychotherapies, mixed well, and came up with a potion that some people on both sides of the Pacific find delightfully palatable. In other words, Morita's system of therapy, though saturated with Japanese thought, is so fundamentally human that it rings true to some non-Japanese as well, provided that the translation of his thought is not cluttered with unnecessary mystification from the so-called inscrutable Orient. That's my job—to describe Morita therapy and the other therapeutic systems in this book so that you can test them against your own experience and decide whether they make sense to you.

If you never feel somewhat tense and uncomfortable when talking with your employer, your foreman, your teacher, your minister, or a stranger; if you don't have the uncomfortable feeling that you should be accomplishing more than you are now; if you have no doubts about yourself, no feelings of inferiority or shyness, then Morita's method is probably of little use to you. It just doesn't resonate in terms of your experience. But if you do need to strengthen your character in one or more of these areas, you might do well to give some serious thought to the Moritist techniques. The Morita therapist would argue that an accurate understanding of his ideas and methods comes about when you give them an experimental trial in everyday living. Furthermore, if the above-mentioned human problems ring true to you, you have already begun to realize that Morita was thinking on a basic human level, not only about the problems of Japanese people.

Overview

Strictly speaking, Morita therapy is practiced by some seventy or eighty therapists in about thirty hospitals and clinics and fifty-six mental health groups scattered throughout Japan. These numbers are small, however, in comparison with the influence Moritist thought has had on the practice of psychotherapy in that country. Just as in the West there are far fewer orthodox psychoanalysts than those who adopt some psychoanalytic ideas and techniques, so we can speak of a widespread acquaintance with, and use of, Moritist methods in the treatment of neurosis in Japan. A recent bibliography cited seventy-four scholarly and popular books and about one thousand articles written in Japanese devoted to the subject since the mid-1920s.

The therapy itself is practiced in several forms. Patients with severe neurotic problems are treated within a hospital setting. Less troublesome symptoms can be treated in outpatient clinics, in mental health groups, or by correspondence.

Moritists may treat depression and psychosis with appropriate medication, using Morita's method as an adjunct therapy, but they find their technique most effective with a class of neuroses called *shinkeishitsu* neuroses. The shinkeishitsu neurotic generally has a strong will and desire to recover, some preoccupation with somatic complaints, and problems relating to other people. More often than not his problems center around an over-sensitivity to others, shyness, feelings of inferiority, and other social tensions called anthropophobia.

A more specialized analysis of diagnosis and patient characteristics can be found in *Morita Psychotherapy* (Reynolds, 1976). Here it is sufficient to point out that the majority of patients treated are young (in their twenties and thirties) and self-conscious. Their fears and worries are of the sort we all have to a lesser degree: "What does my companion think of me?" "Are my faults and tensions obvious to everyone?" "Do others recognize my lack of confidence and skill in certain areas?" "Why don't I accomplish more than I do?" and so forth.

The Therapy Process

Before discussing what Moritists have to say about these common human problems, let us take a look at how they go about the practical business of treating clients in an inpatient setting.

Tracing a typical but fictionalized client, we find that Mr. Tanaka, a twenty-six-year-old male, applies to a Moritist hospital after having read about the therapy in one of the popular Moritist books. Mr. Tanaka is very self-conscious. He lacks self-confidence. He blushes easily, cannot carry on a conversation, and gradually has become so ill at ease in social situations that he cannot go shopping or ride the streetcar. He had to quit work. He is suffering from a common kind of neurosis, for which Morita's technique is especially effective. If Mr. Tanaka were miserable yet getting along at home and at work, he could be treated as an outpatient, in a group, or even by mail.

Mr. Tanaka encounters a therapist who seems to understand his state very well (in fact, the therapist is likely to be an ex-patient himself). With absolute confidence, the therapist tells him that if he follows directions and applies himself, he will be cured. (Later, Mr. Tanaka learns that "cure" has a special meaning when used by Moritists; it does not mean removing symptoms but living productively in spite of them. But more about that later.)

When Morita therapy is practiced on an inpatient basis, the therapist initially gives the patient a brief explanation that his disturbance is fundamentally psychological. He outlines the course of treatment the patient will undergo and allows the patient time to communicate with his family. The patient may have doubts and questions, but he is told to follow the doctor's advice in spite of them, to give the therapy a try.

Gradually, Mr. Tanaka will become convinced that the therapist really does understand and is able to predict the course of his recovery with some degree of accuracy.

The first prediction is promptly encountered. Mr. Tanaka enters one week of isolated bed rest. He is required to lie on a *futon* (Japanese mattress and quilt bedding) in a room by himself. During this period he is not allowed to converse, smoke, read, write, listen to the radio, or engage in any other sort of recreational activity. He is permitted to take three meals a day, bathe once during the week, and take care of other natural and hygienic functions such as going to the bathroom, washing his face (once a day), and brushing his teeth. Mr. Tanaka looks forward to this withdrawal from society, but his therapist predicts that the sorts of experiences he will have will not be so pleasurable at all. He anticipates that for the first few days Mr. Tanaka will drowse, then become increasingly disturbed by his inactivity. Memories and conflicts will arise in him and reach a peak of anguish on about the fourth or fifth day. A gamut of emotions and thoughts will come and go. But Mr. Tanaka must not struggle with them. He must accept them. They will pass. Then,

during the final couple of days, will come increased boredom. Mr. Tanaka will want to become active—to work, play,
look around, walk around the garden. The doctor's predictions are accurate. After the climax of suffering around the
fourth and fifth days, Mr. Tanaka finds himself naturally
motivated toward activity.

Two accounts of the bed rest experience follow. The first I
wrote as I underwent Moritist treatment as a researcher/pa-
tient.

In order to understand more fully the psychotherapeutic technique called isolated bed rest I arranged to undergo the treatment
myself. Dr. T. Suzuki donated his clinic facilities and agreed to
sponsor the research, treating me as he would any patient during
that week's period.

I began bed rest with all sorts of preconceptions and hypotheses,
most of which had to be abandoned on the basis of the experience. I
expected to be placed in a stimulus-deprivationlike setting. Classic
experiments in stimulus deprivation involve blindfolding subjects
and immersing them in lukewarm water, or placing them in bed
with blindfold, earplugs, thick cotton gloves, and other devices to
cut down on external stimulation. In the more extreme sensory deprivation conditions most subjects cannot endure for more than a
few waking hours.

But, lying on the futon mattress in the tatami mat room, I could
see a rose in a vase. I could hear voices, a dog's bark, a distant
radio calling the cadence for national physical exercises each
morning and evening. I could feel the rough tatami, my growing
beard, the soft blanket and cool sheet. Similarly, there were tastes
and smells to engage me—soap, toothpaste, the meals. True, there
was some reduction of sensory input—my senses had to realign
themselves to a simpler plane—but the conditions were not nearly
as extreme as to be called sensory deprivation.

For the first couple of days I dozed and slept day and night. But
by the third and fourth days I became increasingly wakeful, even
at night. I began to realize, experientially, that thoughts bubble to
the surface of my mind, coming from nowhere, receding into nothingness, replaced by other thoughts.

The need to keep some control over the content of my thinking prompted me to begin to review my past from my earliest memories, lingering on each recalled event, holding boredom at bay. By the fifth day I had completed the review of my life and had made a marvelous and deeply moving discovery. I had come to realize that I was the product of the concern and kindness of other people in my life. Life, food, lodging, and the like had been given me by my parents; knowledge had been passed on to me by my family, peers, teachers. Every skill, every possession, every idea that I considered "mine" had been created, developed, or given me by others or by "nothingness." I am not particularly expressive emotionally, but tears of gratitude rolled down my cheeks at this revelation. How much I owe my mentors! How important it is to begin to repay them by passing on what was given to me by others.

The fifth day brings a peak experience of some sort to many persons who undergo isolated bed rest. I didn't expect it. I would have predicted that my rationalistic scholarly detachment would preclude it. But the experience was overwhelming. For the severely neurotic the experience is usually a peak of distress of struggle and, finally, of giving up, but for me it was enlightening, much like a naikan experience (see the second chapter). Yet it occurred before I knew anything about naikan therapy.

On the sixth and seventh days I became increasingly bored. I was eager to be up and active. There were social debts to repay, feelings of gratitude to be expressed, and tasks to be carried out—not the least of which was cleaning the room in which I had been watching dust accumulate for a full week. Despite the inner pressure to be active, I endured the last two days of bed rest as before.

There were no holes in the walls through which others could assure themselves I was "nonbehaving" properly, no hourly checks by a nurse on my behavior. Each morning I stood before Dr. Suzuki. He asked if I was keeping quiet. I replied that I was. With this brief ritual we resealed our pact of mutual responsibility and honesty.

On the final day I was handed a broom and instructed to sweep out the room. What a pleasant experience it was! How good it felt to move my arms in large, purposeful strokes! Although I was somewhat weak, my schedule demanded an immediate return to other tasks.

As I walked out of the clinic the colors and sounds of busy Tokyo burst on me with unprecedented freshness and vitality. It was a kind of rebirth.

The following shorter, retrospective account of the bed rest period is that of a twenty-seven-year-old office clerk with assorted compulsions and obsessions:

I felt as if I came to the state where I would have come to anyway. I attempted in vain to cure myself with my own power. But I have come to the point where I just could not move in any direction on my own. I told myself that I had better stop being obstinate and entrust everything to the doctor. (Koga, 1967, p. 93.)

To return to our hypothetical patient, one of the primary functions of the isolated bed rest period is to force Mr. Tanaka to encounter himself with minimal distraction. He must face himself with all his shortcomings, anxieties, and ruminations. He is instructed to accept whatever feelings and thoughts bubble into his awareness. He learns experientially that waves of emotion come and go, that thoughts follow one another without conscious control, appearing from nothing and disappearing into nothing.

A second function of this period is to teach the patient experientially that the withdrawal from social interaction and activity (which seemed so desirable and "safe" when he entered the week of bed rest) is really an unnatural and eventually uncomfortable experience. The boredom mounts during the last few days of bed rest, so that when Mr. Tanaka is handed a broom and instructed to sweep out the room he undertakes the task with a feeling of wholehearted joy. A kind of rebirth is reflected in the freshness of sensory experience, the sheer pleasure of moving about.

Then the second phase begins; it may last from three days to a week. The patient is shown around the hospital and is then assigned to do light manual tasks; he is also encouraged to find other tasks with which to occupy himself. He is not permitted to associate with the other patients, converse, or leave the hospital. He is allowed to sleep only seven or eight hours a night. He is allowed to read during a specific time period, but the content of his reading may not be frivolous or escapist. As time progresses he is assigned more jobs, such as assisting with cooking, heating the bath, sculpting, knitting, and the like. At first Mr. Tanaka tends to feel refreshed by this activity after his week of ennui. However, a reaction soon sets in; he becomes dissatisfied and may find a reappearance of his distressing symptoms.

Nevertheless, he is to direct his attention to getting the job done. He has been warned that the joy would pass, too, that feelings are changeable, "like the Japanese sky." Life is not to be based on feelings but on productive activity. One can build a sense of self-worth on what he has accomplished, especially on what he has accomplished for others.

The third period also lasts from about three days to one week. The patient is still restricted from associating freely with others and from participating in entertainment. Mr. Tanaka is required to perform rather heavy work, including chopping wood, clearing gutters, gardening, farming, carpentry, and the like. He is given permission to read whatever he likes, regardless of content. He begins to see that he can do work irrespective of what it is or how he feels. He experiences the joy of accomplishing tasks.

There are other elements of treatment throughout the post–bed rest periods that I cannot describe in detail here. Mr. Tanaka begins writing a diary—not about his feelings but only about his daily activities. This diary is read and annotated by the therapist each day. Mr. Tanaka attends lectures, attends informal gatherings, talks privately with his therapist, shares in communal meals, and reads Moritist literature.

The fourth period may be called the life-training period. The patient continues to work. He improves his human relations through sports such as Ping-Pong, volleyball, miniature golf, and through other forms of socialization such as folk dancing. Eventually he is sent on errands off the hospital grounds and participates in group excursions. Finally, he is discharged. His contact with the hospital doesn't necessarily end then, however. He attends ex-patient meetings and outings, and he receives the hospital magazine every few months. Formal hospitalization usually lasts from forty to sixty days.

If we ask Mr. Tanaka how he is getting along, he is likely to say that his symptoms have diminished only a little, but the important thing is that he has learned to work, socialize, and behave normally in spite of them. He is no longer so uptight or hung up on them. Also, he has begun to see his anxiety as part of himself, not as an appended symptom.

For almost all Western psychotherapies, anxiety is an intrusive element, a symptom much like a fever or rash that reflects some underlying problem. The behavior therapies may treat the anxiety itself, thinking of it as the problem (not a reflection of some deeper difficulty, as more analytically oriented therapists consider it to be). But behavior therapists, too, see anxiety as "external and intrusive," something to be erased so that the patient can return to a normal state.

Which of these views is more realistic, most practical, most believable? For me, there are times when "I *am* anxiety" seems a more accurate description of my inner state than "I *feel* anxiety."

What Is Man?

Let us turn now to some of the thinking underlying these therapeutic procedures. We shall give some consideration from a Moritist perspective to what is basic and distinctive about human beings. We think and feel; we make decisions; we plan; we develop; we hope and regret and laugh and blush and work—and we are *aware* of all of these activities. We have a *self-consciousness* that is characteristically human, that allows us to observe ourselves and abstract all these qualities as being typically human.

I am writing now. I hesitate, wondering how best to proceed. The traffic noise outside my window intrudes on my thoughts. I decide to incorporate that awareness into my writing. And so forth. We have the capacity to focus the spotlight of our consciousness on the world "out there," on the task at hand, or on the inner workings of our minds. Let us consider that flow of awareness—that consciousness meandering through time—to be the fundamental aspect of man. After all, what else do I know *except* that stream of thoughts and impressions I call my consciousness?

The thoughts flow from topic to topic, sometimes in smooth transition, sometimes by leaps, sometimes by direction, sometimes in response to an outside stimulus. But they flow. That is important. It is when they stop (fixate) or recycle over and over that we are likely to feel distressed or uncomfortable: when you just couldn't get over thinking about your loved one's death, when your mind went blank during your speech, when your attention kept wandering to that piece of lint on your friend's sweater, when you kept bringing up that missed opportunity, when that word crouched stolidly on the tip of your tongue, when you were so frightened you couldn't think or move.

The illustrations could be multiplied, but the point is that when the stream of consciousness becomes dammed our thoughts back up, eddy around, and cause trouble. One pool the thoughts swirl around in is the pool of self-consciousness. When our thoughts block, we are likely to become sensitive to the blocking; we turn our attention inward toward our own mental misfunction. But this turning inward compounds our difficulties (we're using attention on ourselves rather than on the problems of living at hand) and makes us acutely aware of our discomfort.

What has all this to do with Morita therapy? We have just described the basic difference between the healthy and the unhealthy or the normal and the neurotic state of mind. There is no neurotic person as such, only a mind that is more or less blocked from its natural flow at some given point in time. We are all victims of blocking at one time or another. A person we label "neurotic" in comparison with the rest of us simply blocks more frequently, more strongly, or in response to some unusual situations. We are all more or less neurotic— if you want to use that term—different only in degree, not in kind.

Most of us have had the experience of lying in a warm bed on a cold morning struggling to make ourselves desire to get up. As we lie there during the inner debate, we have already decided. That is, we have decided to lie there indecisively rather than arising. What we know we need to do isn't being done as the struggle proceeds. The sound person awakes and gets up. If he notices at all that he is unwilling and unready, he simply notes it and gets up anyway. This is a skill one can develop. In the long run, it will definitely result in less upset and pain, since it is the struggle itself that is upsetting. Once we are up our attention turns to other tasks at hand, and the "problem" of arising is gone.

Along the same lines, a Morita therapist may tell a patient who has come in complaining of continuous debilitating headaches that there are some simple aspects of himself that he needs to know more about. For example, his nose is in his visual field, yet he takes little or no notice of it as he goes about his daily life. Of course, once this fact is mentioned the patient becomes conscious of his visible nose. (I suspect the reader has, too.) Both sides of it are visible; it is really quite intrusive. The therapist then points out that at the moment the patient's attention focused on his nose he wasn't aware of the headache he came in complaining about. Surprised, the patient almost invariably recognizes that the therapist is right. The goal of therapy thereafter is to so immerse the patient in the needs of the moment that he loses awareness of the symptom, the nagging anxiety, the unappeasable pain. If he sits and ruminates on it, he only exaggerates the problem and inflates its effect on his consciousness.

Total Responsibility

Moritists make a clear distinction between what we feel and what we do. Our moods, our impulses, our inclinations, and our feelings provide genuine flavor to experience; but they are outside our direct control and therefore beyond the scope of our responsibility. What we *do*, on the other hand, is subject to our direct control and therefore *is* our responsibility at all times and under all conditions.

This means that whether or not I feel like writing at this moment, whether I do so or not is my decision. From a Moritist perspective, to excuse my laxity in producing pages by saying to myself, "I wasn't in a creative mood" or "I just didn't feel like it," is neither acceptable nor reasonable. Equally, to deny that I don't feel like writing at the moment is simple dishonesty. And to try to make myself feel creative is folly. No one can make anyone feel creative directly. What, then, am I to do? Simply recognize my lack of emotional readiness to undertake this task at the moment and do it anyway—provided that is what I have decided I need to be doing.

This approach is not as rigid as it may first appear to be. It may be that my mood is signaling me to engage in some other task. That's fine. I must be sufficiently in touch with myself to recognize this kind of resistance to writing. If some other activity is pressing on my mind, I may need to do it before returning to pen and paper. But I shall not be pushed about by my moods. There are windmills to be tilted at, and not just when I am in a tilting mood.

This seemingly harsh approach to the kind of conflict I have just described is most reasonable once one thinks about it carefully. If life holds its greatest satisfactions for me when I'm doing and completing activities I think are important for me to do and if I really cannot control how I feel, then I'd better learn to act regardless of my feelings if I want maximum life satisfaction.

Here the Moritist has already begun to answer the critic who sees him as an emotionless robot of productivity. "Of course I have feelings just as you do," he retorts. "But submitting to my whims or fancies or moods produces no satisfication with myself or with life; such submission produces little other than painful confrontations with reality (deadlines, for example, or periods of sitting around feeling vaguely depressed, trying to decide what I *feel like* doing). Look at your own experience," the Moritist presses: "What has made you feel good about yourself and life? When you've been deeply involved in some activity? When you have completed some project? When you were recognized for your achievements? When you did something for somebody else? More likely than not, feelings of joy, satisfaction, and confidence have come to you as by-products of some *act(s)*, not as the end result of your *seeking* them directly. When you notice joy and try to hang on to it, you will lose it every time."

The Moritist may seem to be moralizing, but his argument is neither more nor less than the introspective observations of many people. Why try to build one's life on the shaky, uncontrollable foundations of feelings? Why not build on *behavior?* There is the source of stability in life, and indirectly, behavior offers some control over feelings as well.

Let us briefly reconsider the business of writing. Few professional writers will tell you that they write only when inspired or only when they "feel like it." Many have a daily routine by which they regulate their writing; they discipline themselves to sit at the typewriter and produce material. If I had waited to be in the mood to write the pages of this book, a good many of them would still be unwritten. Shortly after I sit down to write, my mind conjures up numerous small tasks to be done (plants to water, a picture to hang, newly washed clothes to fold and put away, letters to write at this very moment), recollections of experiences in Japan, books I have bought and have yet to read. Meanwhile, intriguing sounds of life activity drift through the window. Distractions from the time-bound world outside and the timeless world inside flutter into my train of thought. I cannot wait for my mind to be perfectly still, ready to write. I cannot delay until there is perfect silence, ideal lighting, all other tasks completed, and flashing inspiration.

My goal at the moment is to write. I write. Distractions come. They pass through my mind. To struggle with myself, trying to keep them away, is merely to encourage directing even more attention to them. Clinging to my purpose, I write. And, without fail, once the putting of words on paper has begun, there are periods in which I am *only* writing. Distractions have receded, unnoticed. Writing fills my consciousness. This, too, is the essence of Morita therapy. Behavior (writing) is controllable. Stray, drifting thoughts; outside sounds; and moods are not. This book's completion is another reminder of the human ability to direct one's behavioral effort regardless of one's feelings.

When I teach Morita therapy to medical students, I ask them to write a diary. They divide a sheet of paper in half. On one side they write down what they felt like doing at a given moment, their mood, their fancy. Opposite this description of their thoughts and feelings, they write down what they actually did at that moment. There are several reasons for assigning this diary, but one of the essential purposes is to give the students a moment-by-moment sense of the interplay of desires and activities in their lives. We will turn to other aspects of the diaries later; now, it is perhaps best to suggest that from them one can learn that much of daily life is carried out regardless of one's felt needs at a given moment, and even in spite of them. That is, much of life is lived (acted on) because something simply *has to be done*—and not because one feels like doing it. Much is done automatically, without consideration of this moment's feelings.

Again, Morita therapy does not suggest that we live life as

automatons, without regard to our wishes—far from it. We should examine our lives carefully, living each moment effectively and well. Every small action—the way we climb stairs, open a door, enter a room, wash our hands—should be done purposefully and thoughtfully in concert with our deepest long-term needs.

Awareness of, and sensitivity to, our inner states are essential to Morita therapy; such awareness and sensitivity allow us to be properly directed by our ultimate concerns, and not pushed around by momentary whims or feelings. If my occupation requires traveling by air, and doing my work well is an important concern for me, then I must fly regardless of the momentary fright I feel when entering the aircraft and during takeoff and landing. At first, my attention likely shifts among the inner tension, the sweaty palms, the increased heart rate. But with practice the fear is accepted as typical; attention moves to my destination, to finding the proper seat, efficiently putting away the carry-on luggage, pulling out reading and writing material for the trip, learning about the person seated next to me, and so forth. Some of this activity takes effort, conscious control (again, there is no attempt to directly control the fear), but in time the result is decreased discomfort, even enjoyment. Should the fear flash into awareness again, I have the means for handling myself in my behavioral repertoire.

Shinkeishitsu

Morita therapy is particularly effective with a kind of neurosis called *shinkeishitsu*. People who suffer from shinkeishitsu may complain of anything from timidity to insomnia and impotence, from weakness and dizziness to writer's cramp, from difficulty in concentration to generalized anxiety. Various fears are common, too, including the fear of making mistakes, the fear of looking other people in the eye, the fear of leaving one's house, and so forth.

Shinkeishitsu neurosis is thought to develop in the following way. As a result of both inherited factors and situational learning experiences, some persons develop an introversive nervousness that Morita called "hypochondriacal basic tone," a kind of underlying characteristic that colors their view of themselves and their world. The triggering factor that initiates the neurosis need not be such a powerful influence as a lost love or a failed college entrance examination. Small stresses such as those commonly experienced by us in our social existence are often sufficient to trigger the symptoms. For example, one patient developed a fear of losing his breath from the natural physiological changes accompanying a long, hot bath; another developed a fear of blushing after being told he looked well by a friend. Such trifling daily phenomena may activate many symptoms. Clearly, the patient is predisposed to respond to these stimuli in extreme fashion.

We must distinguish carefully here between blushing in public, which is not uncommon, and the *fear* of blushing in public. Only when a person worries about blushing and strives to eliminate it is he classified shinkeishitsu. The typical shinkeishitsu patient is seen as being shy and nervous but also a person with a strong will, strong ambitions, and the need to avoid causing others trouble. He is not satisfied to live passively with his disorder (whether it is blushing, making mistakes, headaches, or whatever). He is bothered by it. He has intense needs to be better than others, to be useful to society, to lead a successful and healthy life. He is possessed of what Morita called "a strong life force." Because he compares his introversive inadequacies with his high ambitions, he is ceaselessly dissatisfied with himself. Such neurotics often arrive at a fairly high educational level.

If it is the hypochondriacal basic tone that is seen to underlie the development of this form of neurosis, it is the psychological mechanism of "antagonistic action of the mind" that is considered to make the symptoms manifest. The term for this mechanism means simply that when we focus anxious attention on some mental or physical problem we become more sensitive to it. This increased sensitivity results in our directing even more worried attention toward it and so forth in a vicious cycle. The patient's attention becomes "fixed" or "caught" *(toraware)* by his problem. For example, a high school student was preparing for the entrance examination of a university. Owing to lack of sleep, he began to feel fatigue as he sat at his desk. He began to worry about whether he would succeed or fail and found it difficult to study. He felt that he should be able to push away the feelings of fatigue and the intruding thoughts by means of his will. So he began concentrating on getting rid of these distressing stimuli. He tried to get rid of the fatigue by resting for a few days, but however long he lay in bed he felt unrested. He tried to forget his worries about passing the examination by engaging in sports and going to the movies, but the burden still remained heavy. The more he struggled with himself, the greater the problem became. The more he fled from his symptoms, the faster they pursued him. Finally, he presented himself to a psychiatrist.

To summarize some of the characteristics of these patients: they have a basically sensitive nature; they react to some triggering experience with efforts to overcome it by their will; they constantly reflect upon and criticize themselves; they compare what ought to be with what is and focus on the former; they enter the vicious cycle of attention and sensitivity; their subjective perspective exaggerates their descriptions of symptoms such as insomnia, loss of appetite, constipation, and so forth; they may be asocial but not antisocial; they show no intellectual disturbance or dulling of feeling. To some degree, each of us can find within ourselves an echo of this constellation of experiences.

Following are case histories of three patients suffering from shinkeishitsu neurosis, presented in the form of the patients' own diary accounts of their experience of Morita therapy, with brief introductory comments.

Case Histories

Case 1. A seventeen-year-old male high school student. This patient's chief complaints were a lack of ability to talk with people comfortably, distraction of attention, insomnia, intense inferiority feelings, and becoming easily fatigued.

Diary opening: "I am nervous by nature. I hear that when I was a baby I used to cry out frightened by any little sound. Since I was a child I have suffered greatly from feelings of isolation, humiliation, and suspicion at home and at school. In my early teens I had already developed many of my symptoms and distortion of character. Now I am bothered by anthropophobia, low efficiency, timidity, anxiety, insomnia, fatigue, as well as such persistent difficulties as mythophobia, pathophobia, inferiority feelings, difficulty in concentrating, tics, body tremors, and a fear of sudden noises. Can someone like me really be helped by Morita therapy? If I find relief it will be a miracle."

First day after absolute bed rest: "I left my bed for the first time. But everyone here is unfamiliar and I am not thinking clearly. When my symptoms emerged as usual, I worried about them alone in my room. After lunch I began to get accustomed to the people's faces, met some people, and worked a little. But I felt anxious about their eyes, as I've felt before. Although the doctor said in his lecture that there is no need to be a great man, I still have an earnest desire to be great. Even now I intend to conquer my neurosis through Morita therapy and then to improve my personality through Zen or yoga. Yet I'm afraid this intention is wrong. Certainly, when I am in a group I enter into rivalry with the others. What a fix I am in! Furthermore, since I am very clumsy how will I be able to do the handicrafts? If I do, my work will be worthless. I am completely lacking in self-assurance. But today's harvest was that by not running away I was able to establish friendly relations with almost all the people here by evening."

Seventh day: "This is the most painful time for me. I must get through this period at any cost and advance toward the future. I am such a contradictory being. I am caught in a circle and cannot stir an inch. Last night I dreamed that I was caught in the web of a gigantic spider. The spider came and said to me, 'It's no use struggling. You can't escape.' The dream reflected my present state of mind. Now I am beginning to look on the bright side of things. If I do as the doctor tells me I will gain something at least, however trifling the gain is. I will let things take their own course."

Thirty-third day: "I filled the oil heater. This was my first time doing it, so I couldn't do it very well. When I finished my hands were stained with oil. Took care of the birds. Today a lovebird egg hatched, two days late. Next I cleaned the garden. Read. Played Ping-Pong. Then I saw my mother off at Takatanobaba Station. I had my watch repaired in a watchmaker's shop. Although I had to struggle with myself to enter the shop, I opened the door in spite of my apprehension. After supper I was visited by Mr. A., a former patient here, and we went into Shinjuku to buy books and have a snack. It was pleasant to see Mr. A. again—it seems so long ago that he was discharged. I felt some self-consciousness, but everything went well. Then I picked up my watch at the watchmaker's shop. Then I delivered a book that I had earlier promised to lend to a fellow patient. She was in the hospital's craftsroom with a number of other women. I have a strong desire to be respected and loved, which is one of the characteristics of anthropophobia. According to Morita therapy I should recognize this strong desire and accept and use it rather than focusing on my symptoms. But I fear that if I do do so I will become passive, stereotypic, and artificial."

Forty-eighth day: "Today I shall end my diary at Koseiin Clinic. I am filled with emotion. I have gradually come to understand the word *arugamama* [accepting one's self, one's symptoms, and reality as they are; lit., "as it is"]. No matter what my ideals, ideas, and feelings may be, it is most important to accept reality. In fact, I can't help responding to reality. Looking at it one way, I am thankful for having been an anthropophobic patient. I have advanced one step, and now I want to go on advancing endlessly. In sum, I dimly begin to realize that this neurosis was like a springboard which enabled me to develop myself. I desire to understand myself fully and then to use that knowledge in a practical way. Thanks to my mastery of life through Morita therapy, I have become aware of my true self now. I find it gratifying that my true self is not so much inferior as it is great. I really thank you for your long-range guidance." (Ohara and Reynolds, n.d.)

Case 2. A nineteen-year-old university student. This diary account, like the one following, is adapted from an article by Dr. Yoshiyuku Koga (1967). The sections in brackets are the therapist's comments written in the patient's diary or brief editorial explanations. This young student was troubled by a pounding heart and a strong fear that he was about to die.

First day after bed rest: "The work of trying to get rid of cobwebs is dull. [We do not do work to enjoy ourselves.] While removing cobwebs, I realized I was a patient and became despondent. I thought I would rather be a tough espionage agent than a weakling patient. [You are not treated here as a patient. You are not given any medicine and are being made to work. How dare you conclude that you prefer to be a spy when you really don't know what a spy is?]"

Second day: "In this morning's lecture, the doctor told us about a patient who cannot sleep well, being disturbed by the ticking of the clock. I, too, was shocked to find the clock ticking very close to my ears last night and felt a little worried. I also recalled having left the bed a number of times to stop the clock because its ticking prevented me from falling asleep. Therefore, I said to myself, 'I won't be able to sleep tonight.' I also said to myself, 'I won't care even if I can't sleep tonight, for I've slept well for more than a week already and started counting the ticking of the clock.' But while I was counting, I must have fallen asleep, for it was morning when I came to. I was greatly pleased when I woke up this morning. I have accomplished one big achievement. I have learned the value of letting things take their natural course. [It is just as wrong to rejoice about having slept well as to be sad about not being able to sleep well. There are nights when you can sleep and there are nights when you cannot sleep. This is life.]

"The doctor says we are not patients. But isn't neurasthenia a condition whereby the nerves are debilitated? However, he attempts to cure us by making us go on our own. Is he trying to prove by his method that my nerves are not debilitated in reality? Can I conclude that my nerves are not debilitated? [There is nothing abnormal with your nerves. You believe incorrectly that your nerves are debilitated and thus you are sick. When a person is upset, his system and his nerves become upset, lose their balance, and function in a manner quite different from those of a person who is calm and normal. But this state is not a state of illness. When you regain your composure and discover that you are wrong in your thinking, you will return to normalcy. The state of surprise or the state of confusion is not the same as the state of illness.] By 'leave it to nature,' I take it to mean 'not to try to escape from something you dislike.' Would it be 'trying to escape' if I tried to live with this 'something I dislike'? [You are wrong here. It is wrong to expect that you are able to flee from something you dislike with the attempt you are making. You should not try to flee from something from which you do not have to flee. You just leave it as it is, you just remain as you are. We train you to do so, because that is the normal state. If you are caught in a fire, you should flee. We never train you to remain where you are when you are caught in a fire. You acquire immunity only after you get a preventive shot, as in the case of an inoculation for typhoid fever. To tolerate something you don't like is like tolerating this typhoid fever shot, even if it hurts. By tolerating something you don't like in this manner, you will get mental immunity to it. After you have gained this mental immunity, you will no longer experience anxiety or fear when you are compelled to face or do something you dislike. You will no longer entertain fear of the kind you used to entertain when you were ignorant of all this. You will become that much wiser through this process.]

"In the morning I took a bath together with the doctor. I was able to immerse myself completely in the bathtub today, but come to think of it, this was the first time I could do so since I do not remember when. I experienced nothing abnormal, but I felt worried that something might happen. Now I intend to take a bath every day, leaving this anxiety as it is. I cleaned the garden in the morning and became tired. An oppressive feeling attacked me around the chest a number of times, but I just kept on working, leaving this feeling as it is. Until now, I used to tell myself that I should not feel this oppressive feeling, that I am all right because my electrocardiogram showed nothing abnormal and the specialist assured me that I was in perfect health. I used to wonder why I should feel this oppressive feeling when there was no reason to feel it. I have come now to think that all this was the cause of the anxiety that made me seek rest. I did not feel too well this morning.

What a miserable coincidence to be asked to take a bath together on a day like this! I did not particularly care for a bath, nor did I really want to have one, but I tried one nevertheless because it was an instruction that came from a doctor to whom I had entrusted myself. He said he would take a bath with me, so in the light of his kindness alone, I could not very well refuse. But I still experience this oppressive feeling every now and then when I am doing work. I experience it even when I am not doing anything. So I experience it anyway in whatever state I am. If that's the case, I'll try to appreciate this agony in full to find out what it is like. This is the way I felt when I took a bath this morning. Partly I was desperate, partly it was a 'trial' I wanted to get through by trusting the doctor.

"When I adopted this frame of mind, I was able to appreciate my agony as I would appreciate a work of art. It appeared very strange to me, but I felt very pleased. [This is the frame of mind that is diametrically opposite to that which a person would have when he is upset or confused. If you are complacent, you can tell what you thought to be a ghost is nothing but a withering plant. You will laugh at the way you ran into your house, forgetting to take your laundry off the clothesline, by being scared of what you took to be a ghost.]

"However, I still have one worry at present. I wonder how and why this fit of oppressive feeling around the chest occurs. Is it due to some change in my body? Is it something pathological? Is it something which modern medicine cannot pin down? I am stricken with this worry. This anxiety does not seem to disappear. [It is important to leave this worry, this anxiety, as it is. You should not attempt to get rid of it. This kind of anxiety is helpful in making possible the early detection of some illness and in preventing disasters that might occur from belated treatment.]"

Fifth day: "My condition improved considerably. Since I had to go to school by all means, I went. I felt my head swimming in the air and experienced the oppressive feeling around the chest all the way as I walked from the hospital to the nearby station. While on the train, I experienced the same kind of worries and agonies I used to experience before I entered the hospital. I felt as if I might flop down a number of times overwhelmed by anxiety.

"However, unlike the way my mind was in the past, my mind today seemed to be in the state of *arugamama* or accepting reality as it is.

"I dropped by at the bank. It was not too much out of the way. Entering the bank, I felt all the strength disappear from one leg. But I kept on walking slowly. I watched myself closely and told myself I could still see things and hear no ringing in the ears yet. All the anxieties and agonies disappeared shortly after I rested for awhile, sitting on the bench in the bank. With all these experiences, I still firmly believe that the agonies I experienced in the train or while walking will never leave me for good. [You are right in your assumption here. Anxieties occur when they occur; they disappear when they disappear. You should absolutely refrain from trying to make them disappear yourself. In our life, worries and reassuring feelings exist side by side. This is life.]

"If the anxieties do not disappear for good, nothing can be done about it, I guess. If that's the case, I'll accept it. I'll accept it because it has been proven to me through my past experience that I will not flop over or die of these fits. [You are making great progress.]

"There is a boy who comes to this hospital in the morning to undergo therapy, and leaves in the evening. He comes every day bringing lunch with him. He cannot enter the hospital, because he doesn't have money for it, I was told. I felt very fortunate to be able to pay my hospital bill. I hope he will get well as quickly as possible, though this has nothing to do with myself. The doctor who is engaged in this kind of profession is a very happy person. I regret not having entered medical school."

Sixth day: "At the morning lecture, the doctor spoke on superstition. I am of the opinion that even believing in superstition is better than believing in no God at all. A patient who can entrust his sickness to God, believing he will be cured, is a happy man. I am certain he will get better sooner than others. [This is wrong. You are greatly mistaken if you thought so. True happiness does not lie in a state where anxieties and agonies do not exist at all. The quickest way to recover from an illness is to have correct insight in the first place. Since superstition prevents correct understanding, it would be sheer luck even if it helped cure the disease quickly.]"

Seventh day: "One week has passed since I left bed. This past week was a week of wonders for me. How greatly my thinking has changed! I'm going to acquire more new knowledge from now on, too. I'm not going to acquire it through my head. I'm going to acquire it through my hands, my feet, and my whole body. There is no place in the world other than this hospital where they train you to absorb knowledge through your whole body. I am going to put into practice hereafter the way to think and the way to look at things which I acquired so far.

"The life I'm leading today is full of life compared with the life I was leading before I entered the hospital. I gained more than one kilogram in weight since I entered the hospital. I ate three bowls of rice this evening. I felt greatly satisfied, loosening my belt."

Fifteenth day: "I went to school today. My condition was not much different from what it was ten days ago. I became exhausted when I completed all the procedural paperwork for returning to school. I felt my head floating in the air. During the train ride back, I felt so relaxed that I dozed off a little. [You should realize that dozing on your train ride back is a reality that is quite different from what you have been experiencing before. But you should also realize that it is not very becoming in a Japanese student to sleep on the train.]"

Seventeenth day: "Before I entered the hospital, I was worried about neurosis, the heavy feeling in the head, and the palpitation fits. But now I've shelved neurosis and am worried about cancer and tetanus. It makes me sad to think that I have to keep on worrying from one subject to another. [This will help you acquire more knowledge, which will be helpful for your self-preservation.]"

Nineteenth day: "Playing table tennis, I slipped and hurt myself. I was careless. I should have been more careful. Since mud got into the wound, I became worried. I waited impatiently for the return of the doctor.

"The doctor once said that 'we should be grateful for our worries, for they are helpful in preventing us from making mistakes.' Nothing can be more true. How worried would I be if I were to be told, on the contrary, to stop worrying about such a trifling matter. We seem to succeed in preventing mistakes by worrying the worries as they are. [You are right. You are making progress.]

"Last night, the doctor said to me, 'let's take a bath together.' When I heard that I replied: 'I don't want to take a bath tonight, for I have a high fever, 39.0 C.' But when he heard me say that, the doctor said: 'What? That can't be. You mean 37.9 C, don't you?' He looked at me with concern in the eyes. Never have I felt happier. Until then, I had the notion that our doctor is too cold toward our complaints. But when I discovered that he is seriously concerned about us, I was overwhelmed with gratitude. I had my temperature taken and found it to be only 36.5 C. The doctor scolded me, saying a person who thinks nothing of causing worry to others just to satisfy his own desire cannot gain the respect or love of others. I regretted what I had said and begged his pardon."

Twenty-fourth day: "I was taught the proper way of using a saw. I'm looking forward to doing some carpentry after I return home. I went out of the hospital to buy some lumber. I felt a little tired, but that did not bother me in the least. One important thing I learned here is to 'take good care of things,' whatever they are. This was something that was lacking in me. You can get the best out of anything depending upon the way you use it."

Forty-sixth day: "In the afternoon I wrote a little about my impressions. I feel that what I learned here will be helpful when I write articles later in life.

"Later I would like to write about 'man.' It can be said that I'm now doing my best to learn what that 'man' is. The day will come, I presume, when I will be writing about Morita therapy. The very thought of it makes me happy. This will be one of the important undertakings in my life, in the life of a man who cannot become a doctor. [An ambitious dream, eh?]"

Fifty-second day: "I changed water for the minnows. As I poured cold water into the water that had become lukewarm, the minnows came to the surface. They appeared to be enjoying the cold water. To those who are suffering from worries, the doctor's teaching is like this refreshing water. I was saved in this manner.

"We have a lot of work to do nowadays. Today I worked, making my hands and feet all dirty. We all looked at each other and smiled, saying ours is a 'soiled youth.' I want to go back to school. I want to do something. I will not run away from any work from now on. I will tackle it. I know that is what I should do." (Koga, 1967, pp. 87–92)

Case 3. A twenty-seven-year-old office clerk. This man was the graduate of a private university. He suffered from a compulsion to pray, fear of imperfection, fear of making mistakes, and fear of being unable to read with ease.

About three years prior to hospitalization he was transferred to a busy section of his office. He began to worry that he had not recorded all the figures correctly when making up accounts and that he had failed to make an entry in some voucher. He began to pray before starting work that he would be able to do the work correctly and perfectly. He got into the habit of redoing the work whenever he failed to get it done exactly the way he wanted it. When reading a book, he would persistently try to make certain that he had grasped and retained all he read, and this self-testing brought about a drop in his reading efficiency. His work efficiency dropped to such an extent that he could not complete his work even by working overtime, and so he got into the habit of taking it back home. He would stay up until one or two in the morning finishing the work he had taken home, and this naturally deprived him of the normal amount of sleep. This loss of sleep in turn caused a further drop in efficiency and compelled him to take sick leave.

First day after bed rest: "When I was daydreaming in my room, the doctor came in and ordered me to clean the windows in the kitchen. I felt fine when I saw the window panes look spick and span as a result of my cleaning. Every time I do some work, I study the result and see if it is well done or not before I move on to the next task. Unless I 'confirm' in this manner, I don't get into the mood to move to the next job. Otherwise anxiety haunts me and I feel suffocated the rest of the day. [You should move on to the next task, carrying with yourself the feeling of anxiety or the feeling of suffocation. Do the subsequent work even if you aren't in the mood to do it. You should not look for any specific feeling of confidence before you do any work. However, it is important that you scan over what you have achieved to check whether you have done it well or whether there was any mistake. But you should avoid checking the results two or three times, just to please yourself. Stop at one overall examination.]"

Second day: "I got up a little late this morning, for I had chills and a slight headache. Then I washed the hospital car with Mr. Abe. I did not move as smoothly as I should today, probably because I was attempting to recall a feeling of self-reassurance. I wonder if I will ever be cured. [For the time being, you should do the work as you think you should, even if you feel clumsy.]"

Third day: "I had to take care of the stove today. When I was washing an iron pot for cooking rice in the sink in the kitchen, the doctor's wife told me to place the pot on an old basin turned upside down. I wondered why she said so and then realized that this would prevent the bottom of the pot from coming into direct contact with the floor of the sink and damaging the sink tiles. With my mind filled with worries, I had not even dreamed of anything like this. But I have come to realize there is no limit to being careful or to entertaining the right kind of alertness. This diary was returned to me awhile ago. I was scared to read the comments, but at the same time, I enjoy reading them. When I was chopping wood to make fuel, I broke a large stone in the garden. I chopped the wood on the stone. I thought the stone would not break, but I wasn't careful enough."

Fifth day: "I cleaned the parlor in preparation for the meeting of Keigaikai, a group of former shinkeishitsu patients, to be held today. I was amazed at the amount of dust that came out of the rug. While cleaning the room, I learned about two plants, nandin and monstera. I was surprised to find how little I knew about plants and animals. [The bigger the surprise, the better it is for you. Discovery is the motivating force of progress.]

"In the afternoon, I proposed making slats to be placed on the floor of the sink because of the experience I had the other day. I got to work on it immediately. I used an old apple box as material and worked on it, still as clumsy as ever. If it had been before I entered the hospital, I would have started this new undertaking only after I had put myself in a frame of mind befitting the particular job.

"I would take this attitude when I studied, read, worked, rested, associated with friends, or saw a movie, because I had decided that the best way to get the most out of these activities was to have the right frame of mind to begin with. But as daily life becomes complicated and busy, I will not have sufficient time to make these preparations. It is impossible to go through this process. Let me explain my attitude by this example. I would not smoke because I enjoyed smoking; I would smoke because I thought it was the best way to prepare myself for the next work to be done.

"But in reality, the more I try to raise my work efficiency by going through these rituals the more my work efficiency drops. And ultimately I come to the point where I cannot make even one more step forward in any direction. [You have been attempting to adjust in your own way the natural movement of your mind. You are running counter to nature and thus will suffer the consequences. You have fallen into the pit which your egocentric personality dug. It reminds me of a story about a man who eventually suffered from too much gold, even though in the beginning he wanted everything that he touched to turn into gold.]"

Ninth day: "Leafing through a book, I came across the case of a man with a morbid obsession to pray. Reading this case, I could visualize how this patient recovered from his agonies and returned to school. I felt tears well up in my eyes. When I was almost through reading, I realized that I had not yet been given permission to read. But at the same time, I was delighted and surprised to find myself having finished the article without any compulsion to pray, as in the past. But when I realized this, it again became difficult for me to read. [When you have your attention fixed on some function, you cannot do work or read books with ease. The best way to read with efficiency is to read something that interests you.]"

Tenth day: "At yesterday's Keigaikai meeting, the doctor in his talk said that when a man has shouldered the cross he should shoulder, God will take over the cross from him. I entered my new life with a pledge that I would make a new start for a better life, but it has been a succession of agonies and tensions ever since. I am exhausted, physically and mentally. Is this because I have shunned shouldering my own cross? [It is not a modest and naive frame of mind to always be seeking for beauty and yearning for some achievement. Depending upon the circumstances, our minds become clouded or turbid. It is only when you utilize your polluted mind and your corrupted thinking as they are for the betterment of yourself that you can say you are carrying your own cross yourself. It is sheer selfishness to hope to behave or act only in the manner your heart wants you to behave or act.]"

Fifteenth day: "In this morning's talk, the doctor said that a shinkeishitsu person is not only greedy but also myopic in his views. He said a person who cannot see correctly even that which is taking place around him is a hopeless case. He also said that although we tend to exaggerate before others the faults and defects we have, particularly those related to our symptoms, we should realize that we have many more faults and defects than we are actually aware of."

Twenty-second day: "In this morning's talk, the doctor said that work in reality is to serve others. To serve is to provide convenience to others. This is the true spirit of service. In work, we should also render service not only to other people but to other objects, too. Rendering service to other objects is to make the best use of them by concentrating our efforts on them and putting aside our selfish emotions. When we do some work, we should not hope to get pleasure or enjoyment out of it but should attempt to do the job the best we can under the circumstances. And the doctor told us that the true spirit of service is to attempt to make things progress as smoothly as possible for the benefit of others without hoping to get some enjoyment or pleasure out of it. We cannot do our work well if we do it with the hope that we will be thought well of by others or with a desire to make money or profit out of it. It is only when we attempt to do the work well by shelving our emotions for awhile that the work will actually progress smoothly. And if it does, we may be able to make a profit or be thought well of by others as a result. The work we do here at the hospital should be done with this kind of mental set.

"We do not engage in work here hoping we can cure our shinkeishitsu through work, or hoping we will be thought well of by the doctor. We clean the garden because it is dirty. We pull out a nail because a nail sticking out in that manner is dangerous. We are told that it is important to do the work here every day in such a way that it will benefit others. A person with a morbid fear of making mistakes ardently hopes to do some work well because he experiences great discomfort when he realizes he has made a mistake. Why does he so ardently desire to do the work well? This is because he wants to be recognized or be thought well of by raising his work efficiency. But he should realize that there is no direct relationship between work and the feeling of pleasure or displeasure associated with it. He should not concern himself with his feelings so long as his work progresses. But a person with a morbid fear of making mistakes is rendering service only to his feelings. The doctor said that such a person is doing work just for his own satisfaction. A person with a morbid fear of being imperfect cannot enjoy working because he is always worried about making a mistake, either when calculating or when making book entries from vouchers. He will always hope to be able to do the work continuously feeling refreshed and without tiring. In other words, he will always be doing work with his mind fixed on his emotions and will not be tackling the work as work. He should, however, do the task by leaving his feelings or emotions as they are and check the result to the extent possible within the time permitted. This is the real way to accomplish one's task.

"This was what I learned by listening to the doctor's talk. Listening to his talk, I felt as if all the haze in my head had blown away. I think it was worthwhile being hospitalized here just to experience what I have experienced today. Today I discovered I weighed sixty kilograms. I am happy.

"Before I entered the hospital, I had hoped I would leave the hospital an entirely different person—a person who could enjoy life every day with all the prior agonies having melted away. But I have come to realize that this kind of radical metamorphosis is impossible. I have come to understand that my present self is my true self; I am what I am. [This thinking is radically different from the thinking you entertained before you entered the hospital. You have grown both mentally and physically. You have now realized that it does no good to attempt to turn an impossibility into a possibility once you have found it to be an impossibility. You can say you have acquired the wisdom to realize that there is a difference between reality and ideals.]"

Thirty-fifth day: "Yesterday morning, when I was carefully considering the remarks about my diary in my room, the doctor came and said that the plum blossoms are in full bloom. The moment I heard this I was startled. I have been looking at the garden through the window every day and haven't noticed there was a plum tree, not to mention plum blossoms in full bloom. What a fool I was not to have noticed such a beautiful phenomenon. I sadly thought I am still far from being cured. [The surprise you experienced is what we call the "first naive impression." This is the first reaction a human being will show to some stimulus. The next reaction is the appreciation of what the stimulus is. The third reaction should be the naive appreciation of beauty, in this case. If you thought you are still far from being cured, that is because you are greedy and perverse.]"

Thirty-seventh day: "Hey, you, shinkeishitsu! Until now, I have disliked you and hated you. I shunned you, I tried to dodge you, I tried to cast you off. But the more I tried to do so, the stronger you would cling to me. Every day was an endless struggle with you. I thought of a sly trick. The idea dawned on me that the best way to face this situation is to marry you, shinkeishitsu. I am not marrying you because I love you. I have decided to marry you because I have come to the conclusion that I cannot get rid of you. If I attack you, I will lose; if I hit you, you knock me down. You are like a golf ball at the end of a rubber string. If I hit you hard, you hit back at me just as hard. Hence, I decided to marry you; it's a marriage of expediency. But now that I am married to you, I will try to live with you and cooperate with you, for doing otherwise would be infidelity that will destroy me."

Fifty-first day: "During yesterday's talk, the doctor explained to us what a cured state is in neurosis. What he said so fit my condition that I felt as if his sharp eyes could see my thoughts. Furthermore, his explanation was complete and very much to the point. In Morita's shinkeishitsu, the symptoms result from the patient's psychological greediness. These symptoms are only fake symptoms—and not real abnormalities—that stem from an erroneous view of himself. There is nothing sick or abnormal about the patient's psyche or body. Since the root cause of the symptoms is an overly strong 'greed to live,' it is not possible to cure the symptoms or to make them disappear.

"We could not make them disappear even if we tried to. Whether the symptoms are there or not has little to do with the true nature of the disease. The symptoms are like a withering plant which an upset mind takes for a ghost. Therefore, if the patient calms down, he will come to see the withering plant as a plant and will no longer be obsessed by ghosts. Irrespective of the symptom, the patient should as much as possible do the best to accomplish every day what he should accomplish, leaving the symptoms, if any, as they are. And the doctor explained that the state of the cure is the state wherein the patient is able to do what his mind demands of him without being influenced by, and irrespective of, any symptoms.

"He also said that a patient is considered cured when he has stopped groping for means to relieve his symptoms in an effort to cure his condition."

Fifty-seventh day: "Today's talk was on the symptoms of shinkeishitsu. The doctor touched upon various Western theories on neurosis, and the talk therefore was very interesting to me. He said that shinkeishitsu, according to Professor Morita, is one type of personality disposition.

"The doctor said also that Morita therapy is very effective in treating shinkeishitsu but is not as effective against other forms of neuroses. He also said that obsessive neurosis will respond best to this treatment, while compulsions motivated by a weak-willed personality are least responsive. It seems that the stronger his 'greed to live'—the desire to distinguish oneself in society, to enjoy long life, to be happy, to be loved, etc.—the more responsive the patient. He said that the environmental factor that helped precipitate the disease was only a trigger and hence had little bearing on the condition as such. He said that it is good for a person to have frustration, because the more the frustration, the more the 'greed to live.' I understood well that a person who has no frustration is a hopeless case, even though many see frustration as the cause of neurosis these days."

Sixtieth day: "If I were to diagnose myself, I would say that I am completely cured. To borrow the expression which Momozo Kurata [a novelist who suffered from shinkeishitsu] used, I can say 'I am cured without being cured.' I can still pinpoint these conditions which I had thought to be symptoms. This is to be expected, because they are the expressions of the worries and anxieties I have for fulfilling my need to live fully.

"These worries and anxieties make me prepare thoroughly for the daily work I have to do. They prevent me from being careless. They are expressions of the desire to grow and to develop. So long as there is a flame from my 'greed to live' there will always be streaks of smoke in the form of various kinds of symptoms. All I have to do now is to get going, by leaving all my symptoms as they are." (Koga, 1967, pp. 92–98)

The Author as Patient

An account of my week of absolute isolated bed rest was presented earlier in this chapter. After the end of that period, at the invitation of the Morita therapists, I lived and worked alongside patients and ex-patients in order to get a sense of their perspective on treatment.

To be quite candid, I was to find the principles and techniques taught within these Japanese settings useful to me in a personal as well as professional way. Let me explain. It is not unusual to encounter some intrapersonal turmoil when trying to adjust to the life-style of another culture. Anthropologists, Peace Corps volunteers, missionaries, businessmen, students, and others who have moved to foreign countries for extended periods have written of the sometimes amusing and often perplexing problems associated with culture shock. I, too, found myself in various troubling situations. My language facility was lacking at first in important areas. The impersonal polite forms of speech I had been taught were sufficiently different from the informal and honorific forms in general use as to make much of what I heard unintelligible. Although I willingly adopted the tasty dishes of the country, my stomach rebelled, churned, and growled in a language understandable to all. The crowded commuter train rides, long hours of work, and extremes of temperature sapped my physical strength.

But it was in the social sphere that I was in greatest distress, and I refer not only to the language problem. In many ways I was more troublesome for the Japanese than a child. A child is not expected to understand and follow custom. But an adult needs a daily display of grown-up competence to support his feelings of self-esteem and confidence. Once, in excitement, I entered a tatami room with my shoes on—a silly blunder. I had trouble carrying on a lengthy conversation and sometimes faked an understanding of what was said, with resulting difficulties. Getting from one hospital to another required lengthy explanations and detailed maps. Finding a house in which to live, getting appropriate medical care for my confused body, obtaining the necessities of living—all these concerns that are readily, almost automatically handled in my native culture required time and effortful concentration during the first months of my stay in Japan.

These experiences dealt reasonably weighty blows to the self-esteem of the then young graduate student doing research in Morita therapy. I simply had no time for these nuisances, yet I could not ignore them. I became mildly paranoid and wondered if the smiles and quiet talk of strangers on the train and psychiatrists in the clinic concerned the blundering of the strange bearded foreigner who was me. I wanted to do well, to appear as a sterling representative of American anthropology, to cause minimal trouble to others. Yet there I was, less than perfect, struggling away at daily living, and struggling with equal difficulty trying to collect solid meaningful data for my dissertation.

As time passed, Morita's notions began to make not only academic, but also experiential, sense to me. I began to see that my desires to be well thought of by others sometimes interfered with my attention to the research task at hand. I became more comfortable with my imperfection, with the reality of my social errors and ignorance, and got on with the business of learning and losing myself in the learning. Much of the inner pressure left as I accepted the feelings of lack of confidence, embarrassment, and stupidity and yet kept on with what needed doing. There was no sudden smoothness to living; a different kind of inner confidence grew, one based not on the requirement that all of my endeavors turn out neatly and laudably but rather on the realization that no matter how they turned out I would be able to keep on endeavoring.

I believe that Morita therapy was helpful in freeing me somewhat from my dependence on social image and impressing others. I was constantly reminded to keep my attention directed toward that which really mattered, what I was doing at that very moment. Perhaps it was not the therapy, only the timing and the situation. Perhaps these insights are only a natural occurrence in the process of growing up. In any case, the growing need not end.

The Author as Therapist

Professor Morita called his therapy a sort of reeducation. Particularly in this case, the boundary between healing and teaching is unclear. In Japan I lectured to patients and patient groups, conducted diary guidance, wrote for Moritist magazines, and was coleader for several outings and retreats. Teaching and life guidance blended together.

Perhaps it would be useful now to describe the counseling and training I have conducted in the United States among westerners during the past few years. Our seminars in Morita therapy at the University of Southern California School of Medicine were conducted twice each year. The formal sessions generally ran two hours per week for six weeks. Aside from assigned readings and lectures, we did role playing of therapy situations, held group discussions of patients under treatment by Morita's methods, conducted attention-focusing exercises, and wrote diaries.

Of course, supervision beyond the six-week period is available for those therapists who choose to try this therapy mode. A description of the successful course of a Western patient treated by Morita therapy (the first patient treated by this means at the Los Angeles County–USC Adult Psychiatric Outpatient Clinic) may be found in Reynolds and Moacanin, "Eastern Therapy: Western Patient" (1977).

Diary Annotations

One of the key features of Morita therapy, a feature easily adapted to Western clients, is the annotated diary. The following are edited diary entries of my medical seminar participants, my Moritist-style written responses, and then brief comments on the responses.

Entry: Sat in seminar and tried to be interested.

Response: A waste of time. If you are interested, you are; if not, you are not. You can control where your eyes are, whether you take notes, whether you sit erectly, and so forth. Then, sometimes, the interest may come.

Comment: Energy must be directed toward controllable behavior. Attention can be indirectly influenced by what we do.

Entry: Following dinner I felt very tired when thinking of all the things I should be doing during the evening. Decided it would be nice to go to bed early.

Response: Sleep can be an escape as well as a time for refreshment. When you need to do so, you will sleep.

Comment: Rather than mulling over the list of tasks, a better tactic is to begin on one, any one, and move on to the next and the next until sleep looms as the most important task. Flight into sleep results in awakening to the same unfinished tasks in the morning.

Entry: The idea of receiving recognition (by self and professor for doing several tasks) gave me an immediate goal and reward.

Response: What if no one else ever noticed your work? What if your plants died? What if the cabinets you have been building burned down with your apartment? Can you found your character on knowing you have done what you needed to do at each moment regardless of the outcome (over which you may have no control at all)?

Comment: Herein lies a key difference between Morita therapy and behavior therapies. It is in the doing that we find purpose and existential satisfaction, according to Morita's ideas, not necessarily in the outcome or result of our acts. An outcome that is outside our control affects us, to be sure, but most importantly it brings another life situation that calls us to respond appropriately and with full attention.

Entry: It occurs to me that perhaps I have neglected the diary because I really felt very unhappy and find it easier to ignore that fact rather than account the day's negative feelings one by one.

Response: Is it somehow "better" to feel happy? More desirable to think and write about positive feelings? You can learn to handle happiness and unhappiness and equanimity when you come to evaluate your life in terms of what you accomplish in each moment.

Comment: Frequently, one finds guilt among persons who are unhappy much of the time. It is as if they have failed to meet some social standard of expectable happiness. From a Moritist perspective, they have failed to involve themselves in life and living. The issue of unhappiness arises only when one reflects upon it, attends to it, withdraws from the stream of living to evaluate the phantom of the self.

Entry: Wondered if my perseverance in the face of such apathy was a sign of self-discipline or obsessive-compulsive tendencies. Decided that at that point it didn't matter much, since I would continue with the work regardless.

Response: Good! How would deciding if it were a sign of either, neither, or both result in getting the work done? To sit and ponder might even delay completion. Why do we need so desperately to know intellectually, to classify?

Comment: Intellectual knowledge ("head" knowledge) can be a hindrance to fruitful living. When self-analysis proceeds to the point at which it interrupts the flow of responding fully to the *now*, it has become a liability. Sometimes the task at hand *is* self-analysis. Then it is appropriately engaged. This young physician knew that self-analysis and classification were useless in this circumstance, so he dismissed them.

Entry: Lightened in mood when I became aware of the sun and the warmth present so early in the day.

Response: Sometimes it is sunny, sometimes cloudy. Can you live equally well on either kind of day?

Comment: Positive, joyful feelings pass away in time, too. While appreciating and accepting these feelings, the aim remains of engaging life directly through one's deeds.

Entry: Wasn't feeling well physically, but understood my need for activity. Ran, swam.

Response: After beginning to swim or run, doesn't the desire to do them usually emerge? Do each with precision; lose yourself in them.

Comment: This entry shows good understanding of Morita's ideas. Without waiting to be in the mood for running and swimming, this person acknowledged the necessity of activity and acted.

Entry: Have gone with the flow and feel filled with life.

Response: This feeling will pass like all the others. When you are not filled with life, when you cannot sense the flow, will you still be able to live constructively, to act with full concentration?

Comment: This is the sign of maturity, to live constructively in rough times as well as in good ones. This response emphasizes the importance of living for the purpose of living, without centering life on one's emotional state.

Entry: Have all these plans in my head for the day. All are senseless, but there nevertheless.

Response: You mean that it *ought not to be*, so you are depressed. But it is!

Comment: Morita therapy does not advise us to move from moment to moment without forethought. On the other hand, rigidly adhering to one's previously worked out schedule in the face of a reality that nullifies the schedule's usefulness is foolishness. The key issue in these entries, however, is not planning, but idealism. The writers resisted the reality that there were plans in their minds. A better tactic is to recognize the plans and go on about responding appropriately to the situation.

Entry: I was a little embarrassed to know so little about the matter and was also anxious about taking the time to read the sales contract thoroughly.

Response: You were concerned with what the salesman was thinking of you. His impression of you is outside your control and is relatively unimportant. Do what is necessary—and so intently that issues like this have no opportunity to enter your mind. But self-conscious or not, cling to your purpose.

Comment: This is an instance of unclear purpose. The next three entries indicate a similar problem with understanding purpose, this time the purpose of writing the diary.

Entry: . . . wondering if the way I am going about the task of writing this diary is the way it was intended.

Response: Concerned about pleasing your professor? Within the limits of your instructions and understanding, do as well as you can—then there is no need for apology. Your purpose was confused. Writing, not pleasing, was your task.

Entry: I am wondering if I am anywhere near the goal Dr. Reynolds had in mind for us with this diary.

Response: All doubts are unnecessary when you have done your best within the knowledge you have. But when you doubt, doubt and keep on writing!

Entry: As I sit here writing, I begin to wonder about the purpose of this diary. What will I learn from it? Will it be therapeutic?

Response: Not unless you learn to write it in order to write it.

Entry: Told myself to stop worrying.

Response: Impossible! When you worry, worry wholeheartedly. Treasure the worry. But lose yourself in constructive activity anyway.

Entry: Nice to see her. Her face reflects the serenity she must feel.

Response: Faces conceal as much as they reveal . . . more, perhaps. Don't aim for serenity. It will elude you. Aim for the controllable, to do well always. Serenity then may come.

Comment: Again, the emphasis is on directing one's energy toward controllable behavior.

Entry: I opted not to study. I think it was a good choice. But it is hard to go back and reason how it was made.

Response: Somehow we know what we need to do each moment. Our problem is most often in doing it. It's not always necessary to understand intellectually why or how. Listen for the need. Then act forthrightly.

Comment: Sometimes I do sense the origins of the knowledge of what needs to be done in this moment; often I do not. But there is always an awareness of the moment's task if I search inwardly for it. And even without this awareness my responses to environmental stimuli often occur appropriately. What a mysterious and wonderful purposefulness we operate within!

Entry: Called some friends to come over for strawberries, but they were just on their way to a recital.

Response: Reality brings disappointments, too. The key to mature living is what you do next.

Comment: When we have done the necessary, we may expect good results. Yet our expectations are not always fulfilled. That is the way life is: moving on into the next moment, a fresh task is at hand.

Entry: I wish I had a better sense of humor.

Response: In other words, I'd like to be perfect but I'm not.

Entry: I became aware of the fact that a lot of what I do and a lot of what I say to people is done so that they will look upon me favorably—so that they will like me, so that they will think I'm a good guy, interesting, witty, sincere. . . .

Response: Welcome to humanity.

Entry: Why should I be anxious?

Response: Perhaps no rational understanding will help. But accepting anxiety as part of yourself—not some removable, extraneous symptom—will help. Perhaps you would be surprised at my perspiration-drenched shirt following a lecture, any lecture. That is me.

Comment: The previous three diary entries exemplify the kind of perfectionistic idealism that underlies both self-improvement and neurotic rumination: "I wish I were . . ."; "If only I were . . ."; "Why must I be . . .?" The Moritist response to such communications may be the admonition to do what is practical to bring about change even while accepting the reality of what is; to expose the idealism underlying the statement; or simply to reveal that faults, lacks, and perfectionism are lodged in everyone's lifestream.

Entry: I found very little to talk to him about and became conscious of this fact. I grew increasingly uncomfortable as I saw that he was expecting me to respond and initiate conversation in a way that I seemed unable to do. I felt that I wanted him to leave. . . .

Response: This is a relatively common human experience. Your attention became divided between your internal events and your guest. When you learn to invest yourself fully in him, when his needs and ideas and behavior fill your mind, there is no room for your own discomfort. "Being" him for awhile will refresh you and educate you. Try it.

Comment: In extreme form this misfocused attention provides the basic self-consciousness of anthropophobia, a neurotic disorder frequently found in Moritist clinics.

There is a meditative posture associated with diary writing. I am indebted to Radmila Moacanin for noticing this effect in one of her patients and pointing it out to me. As the patient quietly reviews his day during the writing, he relives the events at a distance. This nonordinary perspective on his day allows a unique analysis and evaluation that was not possible while he was involved in the moment-by-moment process of living. The overwhelming quality of some patients' experience recedes with the temporal distance during later reflection on the day's events. This personal review of experience allows a calming grasp on the sequences and the wholeness of the day. And of course it forces the client to review his past using the Moritist analytic separation of feelings and thoughts versus behaviors, and as he rereads the annotated diary later, he can interpret the entries according to the written comments.

An interesting suggestion has been to have the advanced client write his own Moritist comments in his diary. After six months or so, the responses have become rather predictable. The stereotypic quality of annotations becomes quite noticeable when one reads the comments of a single therapist in several concurrent patients' diaries. Annotating his own diary would further reinforce the applications of Moritist interpretations to the client's daily life.

Effectiveness

A number of Moritist studies report rates of cured and improved patients in the 90 percent range (Reynolds, 1976). Our work with Western patients has been quite successful, but the numbers of Western patients treated so far are few, and any new therapy tends to be particularly effective at first, in part because of the enthusiasm of the therapists. Remember that for a Morita therapy patient improvement can mean living constructively in spite of the continuing presence of symptoms. Nevertheless, for many patients, getting along is a marvelous improvement in life, and perhaps it is the best any person can hope for.

Suzuki and Suzuki (1977), a father-and-son team, sent out questionnaires to over twelve hundred patients treated at their clinic by Morita therapy during a ten-year period. Nearly three quarters (71 percent) of the former patients returned their questionnaires, and the responses were remarkable. It appears that Morita therapy had its greatest impact on these patients' lives and symptoms within a couple of years *after treatment ended.* It seems that it takes a year or two to fully incorporate the principles of this lifeway into everyday life. Also, the result for nearly all patients turned out to be a decrease or elimination of their neurotic tensions and worries as well as improved behavior.

III
Naikan:
Introspection Therapy

THE SETTING is uncluttered. The client sits, isolated, behind a folding screen in one corner of a large tatami mat room. His assignment at this moment is to meditate on the period of his life when he was in the first few years of grammar school. What did his mother do for him then? What did he do for her? What trouble did he cause her? Specific incidents begin to drift into his awareness: the time she sat by his bed through the night in the hospital; the pennies he took from her purse; the anger that prompted him to threaten to run away. These incidents and others will fall into a pattern of many favors received, little returned, and much trouble and unhappiness caused others in his life. Gratitude and guilt will stir within him and build and dominate until he is driven to go out and repay the unpayable social debt he owes his world. In the meantime, he must reflect more and more deeply. The only relief comes from periodic confessions to the *sensei* (guide), who kneels quietly to listen and assign the time periods and people as objects of the client's meditation.

This is *naikan*. From 5:30 A.M. until 9:00 P.M. every day for a week the client is immersed in himself, meditating on his past. Even his meals are taken in isolation, while meditating.

The introspection is carefully guided. The topics are chosen individually for each client. However, most clients are directed to begin by considering their mother during their preschool years, then their grammar school years, their junior high school period, and so on up to the present in approximately three-year steps. This first topic, "mother," will very probably be reassigned at least once more before the end of the naikan experience. The client's mother, father, sibling(s), teachers, wife, employers, and virtually any significant others are likely subjects for naikan meditation. In addition, such topics as lying, gambling, and drinking may be assigned to clients with problems in those particular areas.

The sensei comes to the client at intervals of from one to two hours during the day. He bows his head to the floor, opens the folding screen, bows again, and asks the client the topic of his current meditation. This ritualized format symbolizes the therapist's humility as he prepares to listen to the client's confession. The client's response is similarly in ritual form. He reports the person and time period of his self-reflection. Then he states his recollections concerning (1) what he received from that person in terms of objects, services, acts of kindness, and so forth; (2) what he returned to that person; and (3) what troubles, inconveniences, deceit, pettiness, and the like he was responsible for in relation to that person. The ideal is to spend about 20 percent of one's meditation time on each of the first two themes and 60 percent on the third theme. Most clients soon fall into the pattern of reporting having received a great deal, returning little, and causing a great deal of trouble and inconvenience to the person upon whom they reflected. This pattern is "proper" naikan. Self-aggrandizement or complaints about treatment received from others are considered self-centered and improper within this setting.

After the week of intensive naikan, the client is encouraged to continue his practice of naikan for an hour or two each day at home.

Deep emotions are stirred by this process, particularly during the week-long intensive meditation period. Tears are common. A restructuring of the client's view of his past occurs along with a reassessment of his self-image and his current social relationships. This reinterpretation of the past is one of the key features of naikan. The past is fixed; we cannot change it. The traumas and failures of my past life cannot be undone. But my understanding of my past can change. I can reorganize my recollections to provide a fresh meaning to my childhood and adult years. Naikan offers a framework and a method for reordering the past.

And when I understand my past properly from the naikan perspective, my fundamental moral self, which was twisted and distorted in the process of growing up, can emerge. But more of that later.

Many clients pass through a number of stages as the week progresses (Takeuchi, 1965; Kitsuse, 1964). Initial difficulties in concentration and a rather bitter view toward significant others is replaced by "the emergence of the real self" with accompanying feelings of regret, guilt, and sorrow over the way the client has treated his loved ones. The client may want to die; he may even voice thoughts of suicide. The next stage is prompted by the sensei's reminder that in spite of his own insensitivity and unkindness to others they loved and cared for him. When he recognizes this, the client feels repentance accompanied by a strong desire to serve and repay others. His motivation develops out of the wellspring of gratitude that erupts from within. Then comes joy, new purpose, and new meaning in life. The reader will note that these stages represent alternations between an inner self-focus and an outer other-focus. This theme of alternation appears in several of the quiet therapies.

In practice, the therapist is not simply a passive listener. He interprets and rephrases the client's statements within a naikan verbal framework. He directs the client away from abstract or vague descriptions of past events and personal suffering. The goal is concrete statements about specific personal experiences seen from a naikan perspective.

The Japanese client who undergoes naikan at the main

Naikan Center in Nara brings an offering of 20,000 yen (about $80), which pays for his room and board for the week. Those who cannot afford it need not pay.

When naikan is practiced among volunteers from prisons and juvenile detention facilities, there is of course no charge. Prisoners practice naikan therapy facing the blank walls of their cells.

The Theory

Naikan theory holds that a person's relationships with others in society are strongly influenced by the development of his relationship with his parents, particularly with his mother. When the love and care received from the mother is appreciated, similar attitudes and acts of others are recognized and reciprocated in a positive, healthy way. In the process of growing up, however, we develop life strategies that emphasize what we can *take* from others. We accept numerous kindnesses without acknowledging, appreciating, or extending them (either in return to or along with others). We begin to see others as tools useful for satisfying our own needs. Thus, our view of human relationships becomes distorted away from the healthy and the satisfying.

Naikan therapists believe that on some level we recognize this self-centeredness, and so we must work to suppress the memories and the realization that would call forth self-reproach, guilt, and lowered self-esteem. That is, we waste mental energy in trying to hold down the recognition of our selfishness and the consequent self-reproof. When we recognize who we are and change our life-style to one of grateful self-sacrifice, a tremendous liberation of energy occurs.

As in most forms of Japanese psychotherapy, failure to make progress is interpreted as a failure of the client. It is never the fault of the method, the therapist, or society. "Resistance" in this setting is rarely interpreted as willful or intentional sabotage of the therapeutic procedures. It is usually expressed as difficulty in concentration, inability to handle the physical limitations of the regimen, and so forth. But the locus of the problem is always seen to be within the client.

Naikan shares several other features with the other forms of Japanese psychotherapy discussed in this book. It emphasizes character development rather than symptom relief. It utilizes self-discipline and a directive, guiding approach. It deemphasizes intellectualization in preference to intuitive and experiential knowledge.

A Brief History

The roots of naikan lie in one sect of Japanese Buddhism—not the Zen sect of warriors and aristocrats, but the Jodo Shinshu sect of the common masses. The Jodo faith emphasizes dependence on Amidha Buddha's love to draw the believer into paradise at death. Shinran, the founder of the sect, promised ten kinds of profit to those who believe. Among them are joyful acceptance of any hardship and the desire to repay others with a joyful heart (Bando, 1962).

One small subsect of Jodo priests practiced a form of naikan as part of the spiritual training for priesthood. However, in addition to introspection they fasted, drank no water, went without sleep, and carried out other kinds of self-deprivation and self-chastisement. Yoshimoto Ishin, a self-made millionaire, discovered the usefulness of naikan during his own search for enlightenment. He eased the physical restrictions and modified the procedure somewhat for laymen.

Nowadays the goal need not be the religious one of an existential confrontation with death; the aim of self-understanding is acceptable. The period of therapy may vary from three to fifteen days or longer. Abstaining from food, water, and sleep is no longer required, although some choose to do so on a voluntary basis. Specific times and persons are assigned for meditation now. One final development initiated by Yoshimoto is the practice of treating more than one client during the same week. In sum, what began as a physically harsh personal spiritual journey with few markers to guide the inner search has become a somewhat less difficult but still demanding therapeutic method for handling neurosis and character disorders.

Interestingly, Yoshimoto now holds that there is no necessary relationship between naikan and Jodo other than the historical one. This stance is reminiscent of the position of the founder of Morita therapy, who denied the obvious relationship between his therapy and Zen (Iwai and Reynolds, 1970; Reynolds, 1969). The intent seems to be to establish the method on a rational/scientific basis rather than on a faith/religious basis.

Mr. Yoshimoto, who made his money in the manufacture of leatherlike goods, decided to offer the benefits of naikan to prison inmates as a first major effort. In 1954 he made a speech at the Nara prison on the value of introspection, and in 1955 the method was adopted on a voluntary basis by some prisoners. Since then nearly 60 percent of the adult prison facilities in Japan have tried naikan at one time or another. Naikan has had fluctuations of favor within the penal system. It reached a low point in 1971, in part because of political maneuvering and in part because of the identification of naikan as a religious pursuit incompatible with the separation of church and state. Prisons report improved rates of recidivism among *naikansha* (client) prisoners up to 64 percent better than prisoners who do not undergo naikan. Of course, those who volunteer for this training are not necessarily representative of a cross-section of the prison population. Kitsuse's work (1964, 1966) focuses on the reformation of criminal offenders. More recently, naikan has been on the rise again in Japan, particularly in juvenile rehabilitation facilities. In an era of reduced sentences, naikan's powerful effect within a short period becomes a prime value.

But naikan is by no means restricted to prison inmates. In 1977 at the Nara Center alone some 1,173 clients were treated. Their complaints ranged from family difficulties to neurotic and psychosomatic problems. The ratio of males to females among these clients has gradually approached equality but is currently 2 to 1. Nearly one half of the clients are

under thirty years old. Records indicate that the deepest naikan is accomplished by those in their forties and fifties, with
women slightly more adept than men. Naikansha under
twenty years of age have trouble introspecting deeply compared with the middle-aged groups.

At present there are several other naikan training centers
in Japan. Two of them are temple based and located in Mie
Prefecture not far from Nara. Senkobo Temple caters to
young male delinquents; Gasshoen Temple is a warm com-
munity of priests, nuns, and laypersons with a majority of
clients who are elderly farm folk, sincere believers in Jodo
Shinshu Buddhism. Naikan facilities in Tokyo focus on families and businessmen; some permit shorter periods of supervised meditation on weekends and weekday evenings. Two
successful psychiatric hospitals in central and southern
Japan have wards devoted to the use of naikan in treating alcoholics and drug addicts.

For a therapy with a history of only some twenty years, a
wealth of literature is already available. Most publications
contain a great deal of verbatim therapy material and case
history data. More than 150 recorded naikan tapes are available to the public.

A Case Study (Murase and Reynolds, n.d.)

Mrs. N., a thirty-two-year-old middle-class housewife, entered the Naikan Center for treatment. Until shortly before
she began naikan she had worked as a primary school teacher. When she came in for treatment, she had been depressed
for some ten months. She became less and less interested in
activities, and she had begun to doubt her ability to accomplish things as she had before. She suffered from insomnia
and had at times thought about committing suicide. Two incidents seemed to have caused her depression: one was a
problem at work following a change in her teaching assignment two years earlier; the second was the discovery that she
was pregnant. Her unexpected pregnancy increased her despair because she was very much afraid of losing her job.

Such a loss would have harsh economic consequences for her family. Before these difficulties, she could recall no serious previous depressions. Medication given prior to naikan treatment had been totally ineffective.

On arriving for treatment Mrs. N. cooperated but in a very passive and almost reluctant manner. For three days she was not deeply involved in meditation but devoted most of her time to uttering self-accusations about her own incapability and worthlessness. She seemed unable to adapt to the situation and was at the point of asking her father to take her back home. Her father, however, strongly encouraged her to continue trying. After the third day, Mrs. N. suddenly began to be able to carry out the practice of naikan. She was able to examine what her mother-in-law had done for her. Following this emotional insight, her whole attitude toward life underwent a drastic change. She found everything shining and bright. Here is an interview from that period:

Mr. Yoshimoto: "What have you been examining?"
Mrs. N. (holding back the tears): "Last year we bought a piano for our daughter. I realize now that this was made possible only by using the money that my mother-in-law had saved. In the past I have forgotten this and thought that I had bought it with my own money, completely forgetting her contribution. I was so egocentric! When she was hospitalized, I visited her only once, bringing her a small gift. (This confession was accompanied by a lot of crying.) When I was hospitalized after delivery of my last child, she visited me almost daily, bringing expensive fruits. She walked up to the fifth floor to see me in spite of her heart condition. At this time she took care of me very, very kindly and really acted like a warm mother. I think about that now, and I am aware at last how self-centered and unaware I have been as a daughter-in-law. I really don't know how I can express my gratitude to her now. I am filled with the feeling that I want to beg her pardon on my knees right now."

She spent the remaining hours of that day reflecting on her relationship with her father-in-law. Again she realized how ungrateful she had been. Thinking about the troubles she had given her father-in-law in the past, she realized that she had not been mature or flexible. She described herself as feeling like a "poisonous snake." She felt a lot of guilt toward people in her home. She worried that she would not be able to bring herself to beg her father-in-law's forgiveness for her faults and imperfections.

On Mrs. N.'s fifth day of naikan exercise, Mr. Yoshimoto felt that in some ways she had become too excited to continue the practice of naikan properly. He therefore asked her father to come and discuss the possibility of taking her back home.

The father, on seeing the drastic change in his daughter, was overwhelmed. They embraced and wept joyous tears. The day following her return home Mrs. N.'s excitement passed, but her improved state of mind continued.

After about two weeks had passed, she became a little depressed, but she overcame the depression by employing naikan exercises at home by herself. Through this method she regained courage and hope. Her rigid attitude toward life changed, and she became more flexible and accepting. She could relate herself to life with gratitude, warmth, and naturalness.

The Author as Patient

As I have noted previously, at various times I have found it useful in my research to adopt the roles of patient and therapist as well as outside observer in order to gain several perspectives from which to view the form of psychotherapy under study.

Some aspects of my experience as a patient appear to be like those of other patients; others are not. When I can provide the reader with information about the typicality or uniqueness of the experience, I shall do so. However, for many details there are, to my knowledge, no systematic data collections relevant to the issue of the idiosyncrasies of the experience. Therefore, much of the description that follows has value only as the case history of one of three westerners (two still living) who have undergone the week-long course of nai- kan therapy in Japan.

I became acquainted with naikan through reading, but like most naikan clients I was stimulated to undergo treat- ment through personal contact with a former client. As with many other situations in Japan involving movement into a new venture, there is reluctance to make a commitment un- less one has (or can create) a personal contact in the new area.

My contact, Takao Murase, a psychologist at Japan's Na- tional Institute of Mental Health, had undergone naikan training twice and had supervised the naikan experience of another client. Regardless of such sterling credentials, any person who has experienced a therapy form has special status as repository of support and information needed by the pro- spective client. Perhaps elsewhere, but certainly in Japan, what is written about a therapy form fails to provide the future client with some important data and may even contra- dict what he will find in practice. What is the sensei like? Is he truly wise? Is he stern? What is an appropriate gift to take in addition to the fee? How strictly are the written rules en- forced? What does one need to take in terms of general cloth- ing, sleepwear, and so forth? What was the naikan experience like? Was it difficult? How was the informant's appetite? Could he sleep well? Were there lasting effects on his char- acter?

Even before entering naikan its influence on my life was noticeable. There was a last-minute spurt of physical activity and escape into fantasy reading before submergence in the quiet, meditative world. Highly motivated information seek- ing about naikan and practical preparations took up several hours in the days preceding my trip to Yoshimoto Sensei's temple-home in Nara. And there was already an element of turning inward as I began thinking about what I would soon be contemplating, that is, I began reflecting about reflecting.

Takao Murase accompanied me from Tokyo to the Naikan
Center in Nara. We arrived at three o'clock on a Sunday
afternoon. The usual course lasts from Sunday evening until
the following Sunday morning. Earlier, we had arranged for
a slightly longer stay. After brief introductions, I was asked
to listen to a set of taped instructions that included excerpts
from a second-grader's naikan training. The tape is commonly played for beginning clients. It is simple and effective in
that the child's questions, difficulties, and responses are in-
genuous and to the point.

Besides the instructions regarding the periodic interview
format, naikan technique, house rules, and so forth, two additional points stand out in my mind. One was that the boy
was unable to recall *meiwaku* (difficulties he had caused
others). He was repeatedly encouraged to examine his past
more deeply. Thus, I learned early that failure to recall inconveniences I had caused others would not be tolerated in
this setting. The second point, that initial boredom and difficulty with naikan meditation would be replaced around the
third day with increased skill and deeper naikan, has important theoretical implications. In fact, this phenomenon does
occur for many clients. This preparatory piece of information not only effectively "inoculates" clients against the dis-
couragement engendered by initial problems in practicing
naikan, but it also builds the sensei's image as an experienced
and knowledgeable guide in this area. One result is, I believe,
increased client suggestibility.

I was taken upstairs at 3:45 P.M. to a large tatami mat
room; assigned a corner; and provided with a tufted cushion,
a flat pillow, a *byobu* (folding screen), and a hanger for my
clothes. I was shown where the sleeping mattresses and cleaning gear were stored and where the toilet and washbasin were
to be found.

I began at 4:05. My thinking was at first vague and dif-
fused, but gradually I began to focus on the period and person assigned to me by Yoshimoto Sensei. At 4:50 the sensei

came for my first *mensetsu* (naikan interview). In the ritualized format of greeting and confession I told him of what I
had received, what I had returned, and the troubles I had
caused my mother during the period before grammar school.
I mentioned, for example, my dislike of margarine. My preference prompted my mother to present expensive butter at
my meals—a kindness I hadn't properly appreciated before. I
specifically did not mention my recollection that she tried
(unsuccessfully) several times to pass off margarine in butter
wrapping as the genuine article. I had begun to slant my description, if not my recollection, of the past. At 5:20 the sensei brought each client his meal on a tray. My sweet potatoes
were covered with butter.

Naikan continued. I could hear children playing outside. A
radio or tape recorder was playing downstairs. Two clients
spoke quietly to one another in disregard of the rule of silence. I was having difficulty remembering the points to be
presented in Japanese at the mensetsu as I moved from memory to memory in English. At 9:05 P.M. we four clients
emerged from behind our screens. We laid out the bedding in
silence. In a few minutes I slept.

Before 5:00 A.M. on Monday, the speaker system high on
the wall of our room erupted with the sounds from a naikan
tape. These tapes contain information about naikan suc-
cesses, excerpts from particularly moving interviews with
clients and their families, songs about mothers, and so forth.
We swept and wiped the room with a damp cloth in silence.
Someone cleaned the toilet. We washed our faces and returned to meditation. At 5:40 the sensei came for his fourth
interview. By that time I had learned a great deal about the
way I anchor the past in my memory. I found that I coded the
past, not so much in terms of the years in which events occurred, but in terms of houses I'd lived in, cars I had ridden
in as a child, jobs I'd held, schools I'd attended, and people
I'd known. The years of junior high school ran together, but
they were distinct from the years of high school and college.

Another tape began at 6:00 A.M. and continued through breakfast until 6:25 A.M. I could hear the sounds of a nearby client flipping the pages of a book and taking notes. The tapes distracted me from my attempts at meditation. I could understand the purpose of the tapes—they provided a model of "proper" naikan, offered hope, suggested topics for the client's self-analysis, broke up the long periods of silence; in addition, they could be purchased later so as to encourage posttreatment continuity during the phase in which the client was advised to practice daily naikan in his home. Yet I found the sometimes tearful and guilt-filled confessions difficult to endure.

At this time my resistance to the introspection took the form that I had somehow balanced the receiving and giving in some relationships and periods and so had forgotten them; in other words, I had been able to achieve a comfortable closure in some relationships and thus had been able to dismiss them from memory.

But the feelings of gratitude toward others began to build as early as this first morning. I noticed my voice becoming softer, even distant, like the voices of those around me.

The screen a few inches from my face symbolized well the sense of being closed up within myself. I began to realize that as I rehearsed what I would say to the sensei at each of his visits I was repeating over and over a perspective on my personal history that was simplified and slanted in the typical naikan fashion.

At 2:05 P.M. a song played over the loudspeaker system linking the goddess Kannonsama with the concept of "mother." The old man in a nearby corner was sniffling audibly. During his next mensetsu I overheard him request only milk for his meals during the remainder of his stay. It is not uncommon for clients to decide to fast during naikan training. During this day I began noticing that I was having optical illusions of movement out of the corner of my eye.

Later in the afternoon a new client arrived and settled

quietly into his corner. At 6:50 on Monday evening Yoshimoto's wife conducted the mensetsu interview, the twelfth
since my coming. The sensei was away delivering a lecture.
Just before this interview I had something of a hallucination
in which I saw golden altarpieces projected in the air nearby.
Perhaps I was beginning to doze at that time.

On the third day I became aware that my voice was rising
in pitch, becoming more childlike. I had some immunity
from the full impact of the broadcasts of naikan tapes because of my limited vocabulary, but the emotion-laden voices
and tears had their impact, as when one hears a baby, any
baby, cry. During the sixteenth visit, after my confession, the
sensei asked whether I felt I had been a good or a bad person
in one relationship. I had trouble deciding. Which was I clos-
est to? he pressed. He obviously wanted and expected me to
say "Bad." And I did. Yet the question lingered in my mind
like an unpleasant aftertaste. It was too simple. Not good or
bad. Both. Westerners, with their decidedly rationalistic approach to existence, have more defenses at their disposal than
the Japanese, who strongly emphasize feeling orientations in
their social relationships. For us, relationships are complex
and motivations are complicated. Was the *act* bad or was *I*
bad? Why did my mother take care of me? Love? Social pressure? Obligation? Or simply without thinking, as part of her
role?

By the afternoon of the third day my self-analysis was at its
deepest. I was remorseful about the periods of wasted energy
and unconcern for others. I saw the need for renewed efforts
in behalf of those around me. I rededicated myself to such
goals. This realization was neither a conversion experience
nor a complete adoption of a naikan view of the world. I
could never see social relationships in the simple black-and-
white way of naikan. On the other hand, the commitment I
did make was not without some emotional accompaniment.
The balance between experiencing and observing is difficult
to maintain. I could see men as puppets but also as their own

puppeteers. The strings of time are at first too long. But they gradually grow shorter, and then too short. That night I dreamed of a clock stopping.

On the fourth day I was still somewhat "high" from my new resolve. In my diary I wrote, "People are to be treasured; I've treated them lightly, haughtily." I determined to make an effort to do more than merely listen to people. I resolved to try to treasure their words.

My ability to recollect the past varied considerably from time to time. But as I maintained a condition of attentive readiness I was able to slip into the deep concentration when "conditions" were ready.

Each day we were given twenty minutes in which to bathe. We were instructed to do naikan as we bathed, ate, worked, and prepared to sleep. Perhaps the daily bath has a symbolic cleansing function within this setting. In the absolute isolated bed rest regime of Morita therapy the patient is allowed only one bath during the week.

• By the end of the fourth day I had begun to drift into fantasies, random thinking, future planning, and mental calculations of various sorts. In the next few days my role as observer dominated my mental activity, and I accomplished only a minimum of naikan reflection. My thinking was becoming increasingly analytic. Were my memories genuine recollections or events I'd been told about later? Why ought a child return favors equally to his parents? Why become stirred up about one's inability to keep his social ledger of years ago balanced? I began to focus my attention on the constant pressure to make me see my past in a prescribed way. In general, I began to react against my initial leaning toward a more naikanlike world view.

I noted that in limited ritualized contexts even small deviations of behavior on the part of the client tend to be noticeable and stereotyped and are therefore meaningful diagnostic indicators to the experienced therapist. The sensei responded to the emotional outbursts on the tapes and to those of my companions with unruffled acceptance, directing the client on to more and deeper naikan.

In the early dawn of the fifth day, before Yoshimoto Sensei's thirty-second visit I sat wondering if naikan meditation on the topic of one's wife, sweetheart, or children might have more impact on Americans than naikan on one's mother or employer. Particularly with regard to employers Americans seem to hold a basic distrust of those in power, whereas many Japanese see their direct supervisors as benevolent figures. Of course, the sensei would disagree with my impression that Americans would be less moved than Japanese when reflecting on their mothers. He holds that in any culture the fundamental social relationship is that between mother and child and that therein lies the fundamental wellspring for guilt and gratitude. Perhaps so; one would suspect that a number of ethologists and psychoanalysts would agree with the primacy of such a relationship. And so would I. The only question is whether or not such a relationship is so separated by time as to make naikan recollection impractical. Apparently, it is not so for the Japanese.

By now, those who had arrived before me had gone, and others had come to do naikan. I was the senior naikansha in the room. Now and again I could hear my fellow clients sobbing.

As I delved into my early years I discovered that settings from my childhood are the settings of some of my dreams in recent years, although the dreams are populated by current acquaintances. From my past, I recalled houses, room arrangements, streets, routes to school, and the like, but I was not nearly as adept at digging out specific acts or relationships.

On the evening of the fifth day I turned my mind loose for awhile—perhaps the best way to describe the process of letting go and observing one's mind operate on its own—and it unreeled a purple-and-lavender undulating flower arrangement, then a sequence with loose associations involving my mother and sister. There were occasional visual illusions both spontaneous and purposefully created. I was becoming increasingly bored. There were small holes in the screen and wall near where I sat. They represented the boredom, curiosity, and needs for stimulation of those who sat doing naikan before me.

Except for the periodic visits by the sensei, there is no checking on the client's use of his time. It is for his own benefit that he is doing naikan. It is assumed that he spends his time wisely in meditation. When he does not, his conscience is likely to bother him. This may prompt him to confess his lax attitude to the sensei and motivate him to do naikan more diligently after that.

Interestingly, both naikan and Morita therapies view the roots of neurosis as self-centeredness or selfishness. Directing one's attention toward serving others is the ultimate goal of both forms of Japanese psychotherapy. Therapists of both types would say they are both individual focused *and* society focused. They contend that most forms of Western insight therapy emphasize the individual to such a degree that Western therapists ignore the basic truth that individual satisfaction can be achieved only when a person is committed to the service of others (as therapists themselves are).

Yet with all this analytical thinking, my diary notes on the sixth day read: "I feel weighted down by all the confessed sins I've heard on the tapes as well as my own thought-over wrongs. Sighs, chest pressure. . . ." On the same day I had a couple of psychic experiences. I had a premonition that there would be an earthquake shortly before one actually began. Perhaps I had felt some prequake tremors without awareness. Perhaps the intuitive warning sense that animals seem to have prior to earthquakes can be developed in man, too. Once, when I heard the telephone ring downstairs, I "knew" that it concerned me. This thought was confirmed by the sensei at his next mensetsu, the forty-fourth. When I could no longer concentrate, I sat listening to the sounds of time passing: a dog's bark, crickets chirping, auto horns, footsteps.

On the sixth night my dreams were confused and varied. I dreamed of my family and of my efforts to flee from a crime organization's plan to watch and kill me. I also dreamed of Yoshimoto sensei asking me, as he did at each mensetsu, what I had been meditating about. There were other dreams. I woke at 1:00 A.M. and had a little difficulty getting back to sleep. As usual we were awakened at 4:50 A.M. on Saturday.

On the morning of the seventh day I looked back with some feeling of accomplishment on the David Reynolds of Monday and Tuesday safely tucked into the past (à la Frankl, 1963). I reflected on the thought that this had been a week in which other people had fought, died, made love, gave birth, argued, and so forth while I sat walled off from the world, existing in my inner world of consciousness for much of the time.

After the fifty-second interview, at 5:40 on Saturday evening, Yoshimoto Sensei asked me if I would like to practice naikan guidance of others. I replied that I would. After observing the sensei interview one client, I interviewed a second. Then I completed two rounds of all the clients. I felt somewhat flattered and pleased to be permitted this experience, but I also felt an overwhelming sense of responsibility. And listening to the utterances of guilt and sorrow from the clients was oppressive and very painful. Who was I to guide someone in this agonizing inner search? For me, as I bowed before each client, the obeisance symbolized not only my respect for him but also my genuine humility as I prepared to listen to his confession.

At 7:30 A.M. on the eighth day I prepared to leave the Naikan Center. I stood in the doorway of the large upstairs room. In three corners I could see screens set up closing off clients in their meditative worlds. In a small voice I told them good-bye and, using the same words that Yoshimoto Sensei pronounced, admonished them to introspect earnestly: "Sayonara . . . Shikkari shirabete kudasai" (Good-bye . . . Please examine yourselves zealously).

The strong glow of gratitude toward others, even strangers, lasted for a few days. I wrote a number of letters to family and friends who meant much to me, thanking them for their contributions to my life. I sent off a number of gifts. The intensity of this feeling state declined over the next few months, but perhaps the effects of adopting a naikan perspective will never completely disappear. I sincerely hope not. It provided me with another reference point to gain perspective on the element of egocentric individualism in Western man.

Effectiveness

Numerous psychological test studies have been carried out with naikan subjects and controls who did not undergo naikan. For example, Yamamoto et al. (1972) report objective test results indicating decreased self-evaluation and increased evaluation of others in forty postnaikan subjects.

Unfortunately, I can find no well-controlled double-blind studies of the therapy's effectiveness, no data on the source of controls in these studies (to know whether they are different in other ways from the naikan subjects), and no reporting of statistical evaluations of differences in experimental group scores compared with control group scores.

There is a wealth of clinical interpretation and evaluation literature, and a number of in-depth studies (using a variety of psychological assessment techniques) of single cases are available to the reader acquainted with the Japanese language. An example of the clinical evaluation literature is Ishida (1969). Ishida sometimes used naikan along with autogenic training and hypnotherapy. He reported over 90 percent effectiveness in treating forty-four neurotic and psychosomatic patients with naikan alone and in conjunction with other therapies.

Using naikan, therapists have reported cures of neuroses; alcoholism; and even physical ailments, including Parkinsonism. Marriage problems, in-law difficulties, school and office troubles seem to improve with the influence of this meditation form. However, relief of these aspects of human suffering are, again, merely circumstantial by-products of the working out of naikan's genuine purpose—changing the client's attitude toward his past, both distant and recent. The gratitude and sense of having been loved in spite of one's errors expresses itself in joyful, self-sacrificing behavior. The ailments may continue. They may require struggle or tolerance, other physical treatment, or adaptation to a restricted life-style. But the context of the suffering is reformed by naikan. One does not—one did not—suffer alone. Naikan promises such discoveries of self. It would appear that to a considerable degree naikan delivers what it offers to the earnest client.

IV
Shadan:
Isolation Therapy

SHADAN THERAPY, also known as *ansei* (rest) therapy, was developed in the years before World War II by a psychiatrist, Narita Katsuro, and his colleague, Hiresaki Tetsu. The latter, in 1975 a forceful and active man at the age of seventy-six, continued in his post as hospital director and staff psychiatrist treating patients daily. As we discussed his ideas, the sharpness and vitality of his mind and character made a strong impression on me. This physician, born in the nineteenth century, could have been a man of fifty!

Hiresaki clearly distinguishes between those aspects of human existence that are panhuman and subject to natural law and those that are cultural and ideological. In the former category he places feelings (of hunger, thirst, and the like); the processes of thinking and remembering; moods; and of course all the physical changes in the brain caused by disease, fatigue, aging, and so forth. We all share or potentially share these aspects of human life. On the other hand, there are the languages, beliefs, standards of beauty, thought *content* (ideas), and specific memories that differ in varying degrees from people to people and from individual to individual.

Why this careful distinction? Hiresaki finds these categories useful in helping to define the proper tasks and procedures psychotherapists should undertake. From his perspective, psychiatrists and psychologists have no business meddling with the beliefs of patients or the content of their thinking. That is the task of educators and social scientists. The psychotherapist appropriately turns to the disorders that are common to human beings and are subject to natural law. In other words, unhealthy thought processes, unhealthy fixation of attention, unhealthy moods, and the like are illnesses in the same way that a cold or measles are illnesses. What is the natural treatment for almost any sickness of the body? Bed rest—not talking for hours with a therapist, not interacting in a group, not group nudity or chanting or exhausting physical labor. The natural process of healing is advanced through resting.

Resting is the mainstay of shadan treatment. The disturbed, the neurotic mind has become exhausted fighting its own disease. It needs rest so it can store up psychic energy for the natural curing process. The patient doesn't need education or directive advice with the aim of mobilizing him. These only serve to stimulate a mind that needs simply to rest.

To round out our view of Hiresaki's way of looking at mental disorders, let us return for a moment to his categories of the natural psychic processes and the cultural/ideological content of a given individual's mind. The former are properly studied and treated by psychologists and psychiatrists; the latter is best handled by social scientists and educators. There is a third category, which encompasses the sense of self, of "I-ness," that is peculiar to each individual. That I-ness, according to Hiresaki, is qualitatively different from psychic processes and content and lies properly within the domain of religion. In sum, then, I am first a brain with associated thought and feeling processes; second, the content of my thinking; and third, a sense of selfhood. The person who needs psychotherapy has a problem with his thought and feeling processes. He needs to rest them.

Procedures

All right, how can the neurotic best quiet his thoughts and feelings? The model is again based on physical illness: bed rest is the key. The mind works harder when there is much stimulus input from the outside world. Hence, isolation in some quiet place is in order. But although isolated bed rest is the central theme of shadan therapy, it does not constitute the whole treatment. There are a number of styles or variations of shadan therapy. There are several shadan practitioners in Japan treating neurotics and juvenile delinquents in different kinds of settings. Each has his preferred style.

For example, the isolation can be in the patient's home, in a hospital, or, if necessary, in a jail cell. On the first day, and sometimes longer, the patient is given nothing to do except lie in bed, eat three meals, and perform his natural elimination functions. Ideally, he should not leave his room during this initial period, but if toilet facilities are outside his room, he must avoid contacting others when using them.

Just as rest without exercise eventually weakens the body, so the mind must be exercised with what the shadan therapist calls "mental work" to avoid sluggishness. Beginning on the second or third day (as late as the eighth day in one style), the patient is given a simple task that takes perhaps twenty minutes to accomplish. He may be asked to copy a page from a book, work simple arithmetic problems, or write a daily diary on both sides of a single page. The therapist silently collects the results during his brief daily visit to check the patient's general condition.

The work gradually increases, to twenty-minute periods during mornings and afternoons for several days, then to thirty minutes twice a day, and so on. The fourth and fifth days seem to be particularly important in this therapy form —and in the others discussed as well. During this period the patient's doubts about this treatment begin to peak. He resists, then finally accepts and progresses toward cure.

The severity of isolation varies considerably. In one style the patient is allowed to take a bath and eat with others beginning on the eighth day and to take a fifteen-minute walk from the tenth to the fifteenth day. In a more strict style the patient is not allowed to talk for thirty days (communicating with his doctor only by notes; even then, he receives no verbal or written reply). He is permitted a five-minute walk on the thirtieth day; he may meet with his family briefly starting on the thirty-fifth day of treatment and may pick up his food tray and clean his room from the fortieth day on.

In the meantime, the daily mental work assignments have progressed from simple arithmetic or copying pages to reading popular works about nature (geography, biology, zoology, etc.) and then to reading about human beings. The principles governing this progression are two: (1) mental work moves gradually from the simple to the complex (with concomitant mental stimulation); (2) mental work is neither recreation nor escape. Thus, novels, television comedies, light magazines, and the like are forbidden. In all styles, casual conversation, arguing and complaining by the patient, and scolding by the therapist are considered stimulating and are forbidden, at least during the first couple of weeks.

Treatment may last from thirty to ninety days, depending on the inclination of the therapist, the diagnosis of the patient, and the patient's progress. In some hospitals the patient may choose his length of stay beyond some minimal suggested period; in others, the therapist puts some maximum limit on the treatment, say fifty days. There are no organized follow-up procedures or group meetings after discharge, as is the case in Morita therapy.

Advantages

Minimal facilities and supervision are required for this treatment form. Shadan can even be conducted in the patient's home. According to shadan therapists, one can carry out this therapy with minimal training and with no personal experience of it, since it actually is the rest and gradual exercising of the mind that result in the cure. Because it follows the physical illness model so closely, it is readily understood by the patient.

Finally, it offers an exploratory but intriguing strategy for handling mental disturbance in that it urges the therapist to deal with the mental functioning itself while only minimally touching on the content of thinking. This attempt to tease out the education from the healing function of modern psychotherapy I find most provocative.

Cautions

Perhaps the greatest caution involves the relatively untested nature of this therapy. It is the least well known and the least practiced of the quiet therapies. I could find no large-scale systematic studies of its effectiveness. Even the published results have not been uniformly convincing in terms of outcome.

In Hiresaki (1968, pp. 389–401) thirteen successfully treated cases are briefly presented with descriptions of changes in their psychological test profiles after therapy. The cases included both males and females, with representative neurotics, addicts, and juvenile delinquents. They ranged in age from a five-year-old problem child to a fifty-one-year-old sociopathic gambler. I found no broader statistics or control groups in this key publication.

A serious caution is that this treatment may be dangerous for psychotic and depressive patients unless they are properly medicated and supervised. Physiological changes brought about by prolonged bed rest should be followed closely. Patients should recognize that they are free to terminate treatment at any time, although it is useful to advise them that the first week will be most difficult and that treatment can be effective only if they can endure the initial period of discomfort and doubt.

Although I have not had direct experience either as patient

or as therapist in shadan therapy, the initial period resembles the week of isolated bed rest in Morita therapy as described in the first chapter.

Case Histories

*Case 1.** Mrs. T. Y. is a fifty-three-year-old housewife. She is basically outgoing but is also quiet, sensitive, and neat. She graduated from a girl's high school and married at age twenty-five. Her husband is upright and gentle; he is a bank employee. The couple has three sons and two daughters.

About ten years earlier, after the birth of their last child, she began to worry about the possibility of leprosy germs in her house. When the family moved to a newly built house five years later, the object she felt might be carrying the germs was moved, too, so she began to worry that perhaps the new home had become contaminated. Because of her fears she gradually stopped doing housework.

She tried to force her husband and children to wash their hands often, and she required them to pour antiseptic fluid on their hands after going to the toilet. When they weren't home she refused to go to the toilet. On the day before going out to shop or whatever, she would sterilize her clothing and put an antiseptic on her head just before leaving the house. She went to a hospital clinic a few times, but, fearing that the health insurance forms were contaminated, she stopped going. Her symptoms continued until finally she was hospitalized.

On admission to the hospital, in addition to the above complaints, she was suffering from insomnia, a condition that had been continued for the previous three months. She considered herself abnormal and wanted at all costs to be freed from her symptoms. She promised to do her best and to observe the restrictions of isolation therapy in the hope of getting well.

---

*Case histories are freely translated from Kaketa et al., 1972.

Following is a selection from the patient's diary (written retrospectively):

"About the second or third day I felt a pressure in my chest, the discomfort of a tightening sensation. From the very first day I suffered from insomnia. When I tried to ignore intruding noises, it just increased their annoyance more. Suddenly, on the third or fourth day my heart started pounding, shaking my body so much I wondered if I were going to die. Realizing what was happening to me, I let out a scream. Then I considered the possibility that this reaction was part of the therapy and worried that by screaming out I had made the therapy fail. Since I couldn't talk with the doctor or nurse about this matter, my anxiety increased greatly. The insomnia continued, and my thinking became muddled. But at that point I realized that curing myself was my own responsibility. I repeatedly told myself that I was stuck in this mess because of my own delusions."

Tenth day: "Tonight I dread the possibility of insomnia. Sometimes my whole body becomes tense with the anticipation of it. I feel drenched with perspiration. What should I think about in order to be able to get to sleep? How can I get rid of this tension?"

Eleventh to thirteenth day: "Will the various troubles I have seem like joys after therapy? If I could only open the window and breathe the fresh air, what a peaceful feeling I might have. When I return again to normal life will my attitude be changed? I wait in anticipation."

Fourteenth day: "As I lay asleep my body became tense somewhere and I awakened. When I am cured to the point of enjoying sleep my strength will eventually return. I want to become a strong person. I am involved in this kind of therapy for my own development. I must use the remaining time well. . . ."

From the seventeenth day Mrs. Y. was assigned letter-copying exercises.

"I have settled down. These days must pass meaningfully as I think of their importance and the reality that they won't return again. I'm pleased that day by day my body feels better. I am continually grateful for each day's pleasures."

Twenty-ninth day: "Suddenly the bad feeling if I didn't wash my hands disappeared. I clearly realized that I am the sort of person who is overly concerned about what others are thinking. But even though I feel more stable, why is my sleep still disturbed?"

Thirty-first day (a short stroll is permitted): "How wide the outdoors feels! I feel that my heart, too, is facing outward. I had only been looking within myself until now. I realize a sense of meaningfulness in this outside world, somehow. I am no longer bothered by the sound of dripping water. I have thought long and hard about my inability to sleep. Perhaps it is my attitude or my thought process, but I just can't understand why I have this problem."

Shortly before the end of therapy: "I've made it through, and on my own. From now on I can forge ahead and do anything. Now my children have reached the proper age for marriage, and I must see them safely married soon."

Case 2. Ms. Y. S. is a thirty-four-year-old former magazine company employee. She is headstrong, stubborn, and given to putting on airs. She is inquisitive and somewhat perfectionistic.

In the second year of high school, Ms. S. noticed her best friend having a long talk with another classmate and became jealous. Then she worried that her friend could tell she was jealous when they talked together later. She worried that perhaps her eyes had given her away. Then she began worrying about meeting other people's eyes in general. She began trembling when in the presence of others. Because of her self-consciousness, she resigned from her position as class officer. She was extremely uncomfortable in the presence of any other person.

In the summer of her senior year in college she took a job examination, but during the interview she was unable to answer questions because she felt her eyes were giving away her feelings to the interviewer. Thus, she failed the examination. She consulted a physician, who prescribed a sedative. The drug relieved her tension. She was able to complete a job examination, including the interview, and was hired. She continued taking the sedative for some ten years.

About six months after graduation she married a boyfriend against the wishes of her father. As the years passed, her sedative dosage increased until she was taking ten pills a day; she took especially high dosages whenever she was going to interact with people. She wanted to stop taking medication and to stop being uncomfortable around other people, and so she began inpatient treatment by Morita therapy, but during treatment she started taking sedatives again and was discharged from the hospital. Although she tried to stop the medication, she felt unable to shake her anxiety without it. She tried a milder tranquilizer, but even when taking twenty pills a day she found it ineffective. In the meantime her husband was admitted to a hospital for alcoholism, and they agreed to a divorce. After that, in order to straighten herself out and become a better employee, she entered Juntendo Hospital and was treated for six months. She improved somewhat and was discharged but could not return to work. Her ex-husband wanted a reconciliation. This led to more suffering, anxiety, a return to the mild tranquilizer, and eventual readmission to the hospital. She was given some medication while hospitalized, but the anxiety and anthropophobia continued and her insomnia persisted. Finally, she was placed on the shadan isolation regimen.

On the fifth or sixth day of isolation Ms. S. was permitted to use the toilet outside her room. Following is a selection from her diary:

"The isolation hasn't been unpleasant for me. It is something I wanted to try. I want to straighten myself out."

Eighth day: "After a week of silence this is a pleasure. I'm tense with excitement. My appetite has increased since entering isolation. Perhaps I'm easygoing, perhaps it's the illness, but I'm waiting for that time when I can say farewell to my symptoms."

Ninth day: "Perhaps Morita therapy would have been all right. That therapy has a reasonable theory one can grasp hold of. If one could live accepting reality 'as it is' what joy would be attainable!"

Eleventh day: "Even though I am 60 to 70 percent cured, recently I feel pessimistic. Death rears its head. In the past I repeatedly enjoyed the mixed blessings of sedatives. I was seduced by them. If I'm not cured by shadan, I think I'll choose to die."

Sixteenth day: "If shadan fails, there is no other path to my salvation. At night when the doctor is making rounds I'm terrified. I feel like pulling something out and slashing it to pieces."

Eighteenth day: "Today the doctor's rounds were not frightening at all. I didn't work myself up for them and wasn't obsessed by them. Perhaps I'm cured. I pray this isn't just a chance happening. I have begun letter copying. Surprisingly, I found that copying characters was interesting. I'm thinking of what will happen after shadan. Needless to say, I won't take any more medication. I feel the courage to endure despite my symptoms. Perhaps that courage comes thanks to shadan. It seems that some change is taking place in some hidden part of me."

Twentieth day: "Yesterday and today my condition continues fairly well. I feel more composed. Today there seems to be a special happiness in having come near the end of the third week of isolation. I'm simply amazed!"

Twenty-first day: "I'm tired of being bored and restricted. I'm waiting for the bothersome doctor and nurse. I want to talk to someone right away. I want to eat with people. I've come to the point of wanting to play table tennis."

Twenty-second day: "Last night I slept soundly. It's unbelievable to sleep so long without a sedative. Gradually my dependency on medication is disappearing."

Twenty-fourth day (assigned reading begins): "Today, too, I feel depressed. I don't want to be around anyone. My anxiety and tension get stronger. This condition is present when I'm reading, too. As my mood sinks my heart pounds. What I read doesn't stick in my mind. The depression changes into anthropophobia; I finally give up and cry. After I settle down only the doubts remain."

Twenty-eighth day: "No miracle is going to occur. I thought I could chase away the suffering, but such thinking has completely drained away. I'm just tired. I want my tranquilizers."

Thirtieth day: "A side effect of shadan is that I seem to be able to sleep. It seems I must pay the price of enduring this difficult therapy in order to be cured of my insomnia."

Thirty-fourth day (a stroll is permitted): "During my walk I met a patient I hadn't seen in awhile. I felt scared and disturbed, but I was surprised to find that my usual symptoms didn't appear. It certainly looks like there has been a great change in me."

Thirty-seventh day: "I was able to go out into the dayroom in spite of my great fear. Compared with my past condition, I'm getting better."

Thirty-eighth day: "I think not much more change is possible. Whether I can make it well on the outside or not, I have to get started."

Thirty-ninth day: "In great fear I started up a conversation. The world has turned out to be charming. Today I sense a big turning point."

Forty-fifth day: "I've been able to sleep. I've been about 80 percent able to break the control medicine had over me. The other 20 percent will go when I get well, I think. The tension still exists, whatever I try to do."

At the time of completion of the shadan phase of her hospitalization Ms. S. was pleased with the improvement in her insomnia but still had some doubts about shadan therapy. She continued to be hesitant about returning to society, feeling anxious about leaving the hospital. After emerging from isolation she chose a job, made living arrangements, and was discharged from the hospital. She considered herself 60 to 70 percent improved by shadan therapy.

Effectiveness

The case illustrations could be multiplied, but I would like here to summarize some themes that appear again and again, particularly in shadan, but in the other therapies as well.

Initially the patients expect a kind of miracle. They anticipate freedom from tension, worries, fears, insomnia. The days pass and they experience some relief, then a return of tension, then relief, then tension again, and so forth. Eventually, there comes a kind of acceptance of the inevitability of the ups and downs of their emotional state. Although the desire to know *why* they suffer may not disappear, their focus begins to shift toward their attitude and behavior *in response to* these feeling cycles. They may be surprised by the pleasure they can get from routine activities. They begin to see the self-centeredness of their former lives, and they begin to take responsibility for their responses to inner and outer stimuli.

After all, no one is directing their responses in shadan. No one is teaching or cajoling or controlling their existence in the way a parent or directive counselor might. There is not even the occasional interpretation of the impassive psychoanalyst or the subtly focusing reflection of the nondirective therapist. Yet changes occur. A social sense begins to strengthen within them. Concerns for the children's upcoming marriages, for an appropriately productive job, begin to emerge. With these concerns comes a parallel desire to be out and about, doing. "These days . . . won't return again," as Mrs. Y. put it. The reality that they have been able to endure a difficult regimen despite their fluctuating feeling states gives the patients some confidence to be able to bear up within the regimen of ordinary daily life.

Although case study materials have been published, I know of no solid research on the effectiveness of shadan as compared with other therapies or with no therapy. However, there is no lack of patients who are willing to testify to the change shadan has made in their lives.

V
Seiza:
Quiet-Sitting Therapy

LIKE SHADAN THERAPY, *seiza* (quiet sitting) aims at utilizing the fundamental healing properties of nature that work through quiet relaxation. Unlike shadan practitioners, however, seiza therapists find rest alone insufficient for cure. The patient must be trained to sit and to breathe properly in order to fully utilize the natural powers that lie within, as they do within us all. The practice of seiza morning and evening for thirty minutes each day seems to be sufficient for many people. Others add a third thirty-minute period at noon. Seiza can be practiced anywhere. Therapists advise their clients to attend group sitting occasionally in order to check their progress and to provide the opportunity for mutual encouragement. I have found short periods of seiza (although using modified sitting posture) helpful throughout the day—in the office, while riding on public transportation, just prior to lecturing, and so forth. An alert but calm state of mind, as is fostered by other meditative therapies as well, extends beyond the actual period of meditation. The ideal would be to maintain this psychological stance continually by means of periodic recharging through, in this case, formal seiza.

The style of seiza with which I am familiar was developed by Okada Torajiro in the early years of this century and is currently practiced by Yokoyama Keigo, director of a hospital in Shizuoka Prefecture. The basic process of seiza, however, can be found in documents in China and Japan written nearly one thousand years ago.

An intermediate figure worth mentioning here is Kobayashi Sanzaburo, the hospital director in Kyoto who adapted
Okada's method for application to neurosis. From adoles-
cence Kobayashi was weak and subject to a host of physical
and personal problems, including various intestinal difficulties, insomnia, and depression. During nearly twenty years of
suffering, he tried medicines and diets with no success, but he
was cured by Okada's method. He began applying the technique to patients with psychological complaints that focused
on their bodies and gradually broadened its application to all
forms of mental difficulties and beyond, to include those
whose goal was self-development. Today cures are claimed
for neuroses, poor appetite, digestive and elimination problems, poor circulation, headaches, stiff neck and shoulders,
and various chronic diseases. Additional positive results are
reported to be common. They include necessary weight gain,
fewer colds, better control of temper, increased patience and
endurance, clearer thinking, and attainment of a more peaceful outlook on life.

Sitting

The sitting position for seiza is shown in Figure 1. The client
sits erect with knees bent and feet crossed and tucked under
his buttocks. Essentially, he rests his buttocks on his instep.
This sitting position is common throughout Japan. It is used
by women in everyday activities and by both sexes on formal
occasions. There are some refinements on this general sitting
position that are peculiar to seiza, however. The back must
not be allowed to bow forward. The spine is tilted forward
slightly; curves in at the small of the back; and bows only at
the shoulders, which are rotated slightly forward. Thus, the
spine forms an S-shaped curve tilted slightly forward on its
axis.

The head is erect but moved forward almost imperceptibly
by the angle of the upper body. The hands are clasped loosely, the right hand holding the thumb of the left, fitting com-

Improper: Back Straight   Improper: Back Bowed

Proper Sitting Position

Foot Position   Hand Position

FIGURE 1. Seiza positions. (Adapted with permission from Yokoyama Kei-go, *Seiza Ryoho*, 1974.)

fortably below the abdomen. Knees are separated by about two fist-widths for males, one for females. Eyes and mouth are closed. The overall sense I get from such a posture is that the forward rounded shoulders, the inward-curving lower spine, the slight forward thrust of the upper body, and the grasped hands form the section of an elongated sphere. If the position were exaggerated somewhat, a balloon resting along the torso would be touched at many points by shoulders, chin, chest, abdomen, and hands.

This sitting position, though difficult to describe, is simple, natural, and relatively comfortable. Two practices increase the comfort. One is the use of a flat pillow to protect the knees and feet. (Anything firm but soft will do, such as a piece of foam rubber, a thick carpet, or sand at the beach.) The other aid to comfort is the practice of raising the body up off the buttocks into a kneeling position for a few minutes whenever the weight of the body has cut off circulation to the feet, causing them to go to sleep. With practice, however, it is quite common to be able to sit in this position for thirty minutes or so with no noticeable discomfort. People with circulation problems can experiment with a second pillow between the buttocks and feet to distribute weight differently and reduce the angle of the knees.

An alternate sitting position that is less efficient and aesthetically less pleasing but more comfortable for westerners as well as for many young Japanese utilizes a chair. One sits forward on the edge of the chair with feet separated slightly and firmly placed on the floor. As in the former position, the spine forms a pronounced S-shape, with shoulders thrust forward somewhat. The head is erect; the hands rest on the lap; and the eyes and mouth remain closed (see Figure 2).

Breathing

Proper breathing is the second key element of seiza. Either of the sitting positions described in the previous section is taken in large part to facilitate proper breathing, and the thought

FIGURE 2. Sitting position for seiza using a chair.

process to be described here is both a consequence of Okada-style breathing and an aid in achieving it. The focus of seiza breathing is a point several inches below the navel, the point at which the center of gravity of the body, the *tanden*, is said to be found. When doing seiza properly, the upper chest does not expand and contract; the shoulders do not rise and fall.

During the inhalation phase the diaphragm moves down as the solar plexus fills with air and is pushed forward. This creates a feeling of pressure in the area below the diaphragm. Then, on exhalation, the solar plexus is allowed to relax slightly while the pressure is maintained in the lower abdomen. The diaphragm naturally moves up as the solar plexus is loosened somewhat. (See Figure 3.) At the moment the air is felt to be exhausted, inhalation begins. Air is again allowed to silently enter the nose, fill the lungs, and swell out the solar plexus. When done skillfully, the inhalation phase takes only one quarter of the time of exhalation.

The critical period of this breathing technique comes during exhalation. Attention is concentrated on the lower abdo-

I. INHALATION PHASE

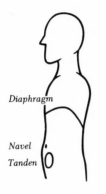 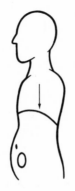 

Diaphragm

Navel

Tanden

A. Rest.

B. Diaphragm moves down. Solar plexus moves forward.

C. Diaphragm moves further down. Steady pressure locked into lower abdomen.

II. EXHALATION PHASE

A. Pressure maintained. Diaphragm begins moving up.

B. Slightly relaxed solar plexus. Diaphragm continues upward movement.

C. Rest.

FIGURE 3. Seiza breathing cycle. (Adapted with permission from Yokoyama Keigo, *Seiza Ryoho*, 1974.)

men. Never forced or strained, the air is slowly, silently exhaled through the nose. As Dr. Yokoyama put it, one should exhale so lightly that if a rabbit's hair were placed on the tip of one's nose it would not blow away.

The steady rhythm of inhaling and exhaling in this manner takes some concentration at first, but in time the mind can drift to the tanden and stay with the pressure there.

For the average person, when breathing normally an inhalation-exhalation cycle will occur about fifteen times a minute. While doing seiza, the cycle slows to about six or seven times a minute. Advanced practitioners reduce the frequency to as low as two or three times a minute and lower. The aim for the beginner is not to reduce the number of breath cycles per minute quickly but to achieve the maximum in proper expansion and contraction within the range of comfort, without strain.

Now we can see the sense behind the sitting position. The knees are down out of the way, not interfering with the forward thrust of the solar plexus or lower abdomen. The shoulders are forward, encouraging the air to move down rather than fill the expanded upper lungs, as would be the case if the shoulders were pulled back.

Experiment with your own shoulders forward and then back, your own knees up close to your chest and then in a normal sitting position, and finally in a kneeling position. Doing this will give you some experiential sense of the reasonableness of the seiza posture for abdominal breathing.

Thought Process

While doing seiza, the beginner usually finds himself absorbed in the process of maintaining proper posture and breathing. There may be initial discomfort in the legs and back, although I find the sitting position of seiza more comfortable than that of *zazen* (Zen sitting).

Concentration should focus on the breaths, one by one. Distractions are handled in seiza as they are in most meditative therapies. The meditator is not to struggle with stray thoughts or intruding sensations. He should not try to get rid of them, nor should he try to close his mind to keep them out. Rather, he must accept them, allow them to pass through his attention as he constantly swings the focus of his consciousness back to the breathing itself.

Close your eyes for a few moments and try not to think about the sounds that enter your field of hearing right now. Many readers will find that the more they try to block off their hearing, the more sensitive they will be to the sounds they are trying to exclude from their awareness.

But, as your attention returns to this book, the sounds will gradually fade away and the content of the written material will fill the foreground of your consciousness. The aim of seiza is to fill the consciousness with the immediate rhythmic breathing.

The client is not asleep or hypnotized. He is absorbed in the quieting inner world of a basic biological process. He is not passively resigned to some inexorable fate, nor tuned out from reality. Rather, he is tuned in to an ongoing inner reality through an exercise that is designed to leave him better able to respond to the composite of inner and outer worlds that make up his everyday phenomenological reality.

Physiological Changes

It is difficult to assess the changes that take place in the mind of a person doing seiza. Interrupting his meditation in order to ask him about the shifting state of his mind would be artificial and disruptive. Moreover, he may not be aware of changes in his attitude and orientation toward himself and his world.

It is possible, however, to use instruments to continuously monitor certain physiological signs during seiza and to note consistent changes that appear in nearly all clients. Seiza meditators often report experiencing sensations of warm hands and feet, a cool forehead, and increased salivation.

The instruments confirm these self-reports. Yokoyama has reported findings of lowered pulse, lowered blood pressure (particularly in persons with high initial blood pressure), lowered temperature under the tongue and at the forehead, increased circulation and warming of extremities, and increased salivation. As in zazen, the expenditure of body energy probably decreases some 10 to 20 percent.

Changing Perspectives

As in most meditative therapies, the new client may be attracted by the hope of curing his neurosis, overcoming his fears and self-doubts, improving his physical health, or developing his character. In time, however, he learns that those were immature fantasies. The purpose of seiza is simply to sit quietly. This concept may seem strange at first. Yet in various forms it is an essential ingredient of many Japanese psychotherapies. What does it mean to sit only for the purpose of sitting? What about the goals of self-development, overcoming fears and compulsions, feeling better?

Let me try to explain my understanding of this apparent paradox. The essence of our desire to improve ourselves, to erase fears and compulsions, to have better health and better dispositions, to feel more confident and self-assured—the core of all these aspirations—is a dissatisfaction with what *is* and a desire for what *might be* or what *ought to be*. If this conflict between the real and the ideal could be resolved, the unnecessary unhappiness and anxiety would disappear. But the more we try to overcome the discrepancy or conflict, the more we are caught in the act of trying to overcome it. As when trying to get free from flypaper, the more we try to shake and pull free from the dilemma, the more we are caught in it. The solution offered by many Japanese therapies, in one form or another, is to stop trying to overcome the conflict, but to accept reality by doing. In seiza, the doing is quiet sitting. Sitting is a microcosm of the orientation that one can develop toward life. There are many other activities the client could be engaged in during the time he is sitting. But he sits. His thoughts could be flitting from topic to topic, and sometimes they do; sometimes they focus on his own breathing and posture. Is the investment of his time and awareness in sitting worth it? Compared with what he might be doing or thinking, is the sitting experience valuable? Still he sits. He may sit initially because of hopes of cure; he may continue because of social pressure; but in the end he is likely to arrive at a simple acceptance that he is sitting. His mind becomes less cluttered by the "mights" and "coulds" and "ought-to-bes." He simply sits.

Extend this orientation to eating, walking, defecating, typing, talking, sleeping, bathing—to every aspect of life—and a kind of freedom and serenity emerges. The goals do not disappear entirely. I may walk knowing where I am headed and why I am going there. But even the goals are now accepted as part of my reality. There is no wishing that I had this goal instead of that one, and even if there were, there would be acceptance of the wishing, and so forth. The purpose of sitting is to sit. And when it isn't, it isn't.

Case Histories

Case 1. Mr. K. T., a middle-aged teacher, had been taking sleeping prescriptions and tranquilizers for ten years but still complained of insomnia. He attended seiza sessions for four months as an outpatient and continued to take medication but found little relief. He was subsequently admitted to a hospital specializing in seiza, stopped his dependence on sleep medicine, and within three weeks was sleeping regularly and well.

A year after discharge he wrote:

If I hadn't learned about seiza I don't know where I'd be now. It has only been about a year since I began seiza, but my life has completely changed. Until then, unless I took two or more kinds of sleeping pill I could never sleep. For over ten years I had used sleep medicine and had reached a state of drug dependence, yet exactly a week after I began seiza in the hospital I slept soundly by preparing myself with an hour of seiza sitting.

Since my discharge I arise promptly at 6:00 A.M. It's marvelous! My life now involves eating breakfast and getting to work on time. In fact, lately I've been the first to arrive, even commuting leisurely. Perhaps it's not worth mentioning, but getting up at 6:00 A.M. without strain is a radical change from my previous life-style. Nowadays the busier I am, the happier and healthier I feel. My weight has increased by eleven kilograms. Seiza has brought a new perspective on life, a series of splendid bright mornings. I feel it is safe to say that seiza is my life itself.

Case 2. M. H., the fifty-eight-year-old wife of a Zen Buddhist priest, was admitted to Ushibuse Hospital suffering from an obsessive fear of cancer and resulting sleeplessness.

She had been operated on three years earlier because of a polyp on her stomach. After that, because of insomnia and extreme anxiety about cancer, she returned to Ushibuse Hospital many times. After one week of Morita therapy's absolute, isolated bed rest at the hospital she began doing seiza. Within a couple of days her phobia disappeared, and she began to accept her insomnia without struggling. She wrote about this abrupt change:

On July 27 I didn't sleep a wink and morning dawned. I got up dizzily. How can I make it through the day? I wondered as I washed my face. Without any eagerness I attended the seiza session. I don't remember how long I sat at seiza, but I was not uncomfortable. A marvelous thing—a fresh, renewed feeling emerged! I felt I could do a little, so I did some cleaning. It was not difficult. I cut grass and accomplished that task. I felt as if I had slept after all. Fine! After last night's misery, today was turned into joy.

On the twenty-eighth I realized that yesterday was a turning point in my life. Even though I didn't sleep last night I wasn't upset by it. Sleep or not, it's all right, I thought. Anyway, even without sleep I'll enjoy working all day. And the relaxed feeling will help me sleep tonight. After the morning seiza I felt inexpressibly happy. Until yesterday I had felt I would eventually die in this hospital, but after returning from seiza there seemed to be light in the dark cloud in which I had been existing. My body felt suddenly different; it was as if a new self has been created. The condition of my stomach was improved, too, and I worked happily all day. With only the two seiza sessions yesterday morning and evening, the fears I had been carrying around for such a long time were cut away. If seiza were a medicine, I needed only two doses of it to be cured. I don't know about tomorrow, but I am living fully today. The raw vegetables—cucumbers, cabbage, and the like—which I couldn't eat before I ate with gusto yesterday and today, with no ill effects. I haven't eaten such food for years. This morning I entered the bath and washed away the dust from my body and spirit. What a satisfying feeling this is!

Effectiveness

Yokoyama Keigo sent a questionnaire to 357 former patients whom he had treated with seiza for neurotic and psychosomatic complaints during a ten-year period. Of the 303 who replied, nearly three quarters of them said they were completely cured (they either had no symptoms or were not bothered by them); and with the exception of 11 persons still suffering and unable to function, the remaining quarter were able to lead a normal life in spite of their symptoms and their anxieties about them.

These ex-patients attributed the following gains to seiza: increased calm (207 respondents), better appetite (123), decreased insomnia (122), weight gain (99), better control of temper (97), fewer eliminative problems (96), fewer colds (70), and so on down the long list from higher efficiency at work to fewer headaches.

The caution about evaluative effectiveness of any treatment noted in the Preface holds here, but clearly some patients attribute substantial gains to seiza.

My own experience is that the sitting position of seiza feels quite comfortable for periods of up to thirty or forty minutes.

The inner experience that accompanies seiza seems not unlike that which comes with counting breaths in zazen. I sense
a gradual stilling of mental processes, a settling or grounding
of my consciousness, a dynamic peacefulness. During the
first ten to fifteen minutes, thoughts, recollections, and plans
float into my awareness. Those that seem important or recur-
ring I note on a tablet and consider later. The others I successfully dismiss at the moment. After this initial effort of the
everyday consciousness to assert itself, my mind drifts into
calmer waters, and the focus on breathing continues relatively undisturbed. From discussions with others who practice
seiza regularly and for longer periods than I do, extended
practice brings about an earlier entry into a deeper level of
meditation and produces even more energy and noticeably
improved personal stability.

VI
Zen:
Meditation Therapy

WHY HAVE I INCLUDED ZEN in a collection of descriptions of Japanese psychotherapies? Isn't it a religion? Certainly that is the way many westerners think of it—a sort of esoteric religious tradition of the East. You have probably read of monks who spent years concentrating on koans, riddles with no rational answer, such as "What is the sound of one hand clapping?"

Interestingly, the Japanese take a much more practical view of the practice of Zen. Zen is seen by many Japanese as a form of self-discipline, a means of achieving better physical and mental health, an art with cultural and historical depth. A number of the patients I met as they underwent Morita therapy or seiza or naikan had previously tried *zazen* (Zen sitting) to cure their anxieties, fears, compulsions, and psychosomatic symptoms. Among Zen laymen and priests I met several who exhibited obvious mental difficulties, and I met others who had been cured through Zen. Many people practice Zen sitting simply to strengthen and deepen their character. When asked about the reasons people come to do Zen sitting at his temple, one *roshi* (Zen master) replied, "Most of the people who come here are students who, for the most part, are merely restless. They want *hara* [lit., "abdomen", a sort of composure]. Then there are neurotics who come accompanied by their protectors, and older people who are troubled in one way or another. Many come simply for the calm; others, university lecturers, for example, because they are not able to find as much in other religions" (Stryk and Ikemoto, 1965, pp. 154–155).

The philosophical underpinnings of Zen, Morita therapy, and seiza are so similar that combinations of Morita therapy along with Zen sitting or seiza are practiced by several Morita therapists.

In this chapter I shall focus on the practice of zazen and touch only lightly the larger subjects of Zen philosophy and the total life context in which zazen is practiced. However, in order to make some sense of the practice of zazen, we must take a brief look at the Zen world view.

Zen Theory

To gain an overview of Zen thought, let's examine the following illustrative exchange: "Boy, am I hungry . . . boy, am I hungry . . . boy, am I hungry." "Here, have some food." "Thanks. . . . Boy, was I hungry."

The first and most basic question involved here is, "Who is the 'I' that is hungry?" This sounds like a philosophical issue, and I suppose it is on one level. There is another way to answer the question, however, a way that doesn't involve philosophical thinking or argument. That way is to sit in zazen until the "I" evaporates or expands or shrinks or otherwise reveals its essential nothingness. I cannot fully explain what I mean by this; like others who have experienced zazen, I can only point the way toward discovering it.

Now, what has this to do with therapy? The basic problem that is dealt with in any psychotherapy for neurosis begins with "*I* am hurting." The client comes for therapy because he feels his dis-ease, his discomfort, his suffering: "*I* am troubled." "*I* need help." "*I* can't go on like this."

Long ago in China a man asked a kind of therapist, "I beg you, Master, let me have peace of mind." The reply was, "Bring me your mind and I will put it at ease." "But even though I look for my mind, I cannot grasp hold of it." "There, I have just put it at ease."

The "therapist" in this situation was not offering double-talk. He was pointing out a realistic difficulty in his patient's complaint. Did the patient bring a troubled mind for cure, or was he simply experiencing trouble? " 'I' cannot grasp hold of 'it.' " The patient talked as if there were a self, "I," and a mind, "it." What if there were only one, or neither? I would argue that a more accurate verbal description of the patient's problem is the following: there exists a dis-ease.

When the therapist posed a critical problem—"Bring me your mind . . ."—the patient had to think about obeying and found that he could not comply. In the moment of trying to meet the therapist's demand, the dis-ease disappeared. Why? There is nothing *occult* here. He simply focused his attention on trying to solve the problem of the moment and in so doing forgot his dis-ease.

This description is rather sloppy because language pushes us to write as if the dis-ease were still there, only forgotten as he concentrated on the impossible task of bringing his mind to the therapist. Language also forces us to use the word "he" as a locator of where the dis-ease and the concentration are. In fact, of course, I cannot locate my discomfort or joy in space; I can't point to it. Nor can I point to my mind (not my brain, my mind—they are quite different "things") or to me (not to my body, to me).

At any rate, there was discomfort, redirected attention, and the recognition that the discomfort was gone. Our first lesson from the illustration is that the "I" in "Boy, am I hungry," is open to some question. The experience of hunger surely exists. But what is this "I" that is hungry?

The second lesson is the obsession with the hunger, even after it was gone. "Boy, was I hungry." A person who is fully functioning is alive to each moment. He cannot be caught by the hunger that was but is no more. There are numerous Zen stories about this principle. For example, a junior and senior priest were walking past a bakery. The aroma of baking bread drifted into the street. "What a lovely smell," the junior priest noted. "It certainly is." A few blocks later the junior monk remarked again, "The odor from that bakery makes me want to eat some bread." "What bakery?"

The senior monk's mind had moved on. In another story a Zen priest and his disciple came to a stream. There, a lovely young lady was in a quandary because the bridge had been washed away and she could not cross the stream. The priest gathered up his robe, picked her up, and waded to the opposite bank. Then he and his disciple continued traveling. After awhile, the disciple asked if his master had endangered his vows of chastity by carrying the maiden across the water. "Are you still carrying her? I sat her down on the bank as soon as we crossed the stream," was the reply.

How much of our lives is spent in reverie, in wishing for what cannot be, in regretting what might have been avoided. These obsessions steal from us the moments of the *now*.

There is a final lesson I want to glean from our illustrations. It is the lesson of giving. "Here, have some food." One of the great difficulties I had in understanding Zen was why it should produce people who played by the rules of society. If Zen is such a freeing discipline, why should the priests come down from their temples to serve humanity? Why should banks and other companies send their employees to Zen temples for spiritual training? If I learn that "I" am a social fiction and so are "you," that we are part of a great Oneness, that it is an illusion to think "this is good," "this is bad," then why should anyone choose to serve an illusory mankind according to some illusory standards of goodness?

I think that part of the concern for others is maintained by the camaraderie of those practicing Zen together and the personal relationship between the disciple and the roshi who guides him. Those who enter a monastery to become Zen priests recite daily vows to serve humanity. And there seems to be something about the meditative experience itself that, in these settings, promotes a willingness (not a drive) to give to others. If this explanation appears vague, it is because I do not yet fully understand this paradox of freedom and service. But its existence is worth pointing out.

Paul Wienpahl provides us with his interpretation of a dogmatic, then an experiential, resolution of this same paradox. "I am here because of my parents and they because of theirs. . . . All this past effort is crystallized in each of us. . . . I eat rice which is grown by this man, wear clothes made by those men, and so on. . . . So the Zen attitude is to bow in all directions to give thanks to all. And if you understand this gratitude you try to serve society" (Wienpahl, 1970, p. 192).

"There are, if you will, two major ways of experiencing life. In the one we are separate and alone. It is the dualistic way, and it has its function. In the other we are everything. In it our responsibility is seen to be so complete that it is natural. It is natural to revere and to help every thing and being, because it is natural to help oneself" (Wienpahl, 1970, p. 233).

Zen Practice: Therapy

As we find in the other quiet therapies, Zen emphasizes the experiential aspect of practice over theory. D. T. Suzuki put it this way: "However much we may talk about water and describe it quite intelligently, that does not make it real water. So with fire. Mere talking of it will not make the mouth burn. To know what they are means to experience them in actual concreteness. A book on cooking will not cure our hunger. To feel satisfied we must have actual food. So long as we do not go beyond mere talking, we are not true knowers" (Suzuki, 1959, p. 104).

The techniques of Zen are rather simple to learn *about*. But they take dedicated practice before they yield experiential understanding and desired results. As in typing, one can easily learn *about* the touch-type system, but that is a far cry from being able to type well at the rate of 75 words per minute.

Zazen is the practice essential to experiencing Zen. There

are styles of zazen and extensions of zazen, but before taking note of them we must reiterate the difference between the dual thrusts of Zen as religion and Zen as therapy. On the latter level, the client aims at developing concentration, mental power, stability of character, and improvement of health. On the religious level, he aims at realizing his true nature and that of the universe. (The focus of this book is on the therapeutic function; the enlightenment aspect will be mentioned only for comparative purposes.)

As for the practice of zazen, there are no simpler and clearer instructions than those offered by Dogen, the founder of a Zen sect, over seven hundred years ago:

"For this meditation a quiet chamber is necessary, while food and drink must be taken in moderation. Free yourself from all attachments, and bring to rest the ten thousand things. Think of neither good nor evil and judge not right or wrong. Maintain the flow of mind, of will, and of consciousness; bring to an end all desires, all concepts and judgments. Do not think about how to become a Buddha.

"In terms of procedure, first put down a thick pillow and on top of this a second (round) one. One may choose either a full or half cross-legged position. In the full postion one places the right foot on the left thigh and the left foot on the right thigh. In the half position only the left foot is placed upon the right thigh. Robe and belt should be worn loosely, but in order. The right hand rests on the left foot, while the back of the left hand rests in the palm of the right. The two thumbs are placed in juxtaposition.

"The body must be maintained upright, without inclining to the left or to the right, forward or backward. Ears and shoulders, nose and navel must be kept in alignment respectively. The tongue is to be kept against the palate, lips and teeth are kept firmly closed, while the eyes are to be kept always open.

"Now that the bodily position is in order, regulate your breathing. If a wish arises, take note of it and then dismiss it.

In practicing thus persistently you will forget all attachments and concentration will come of itself. That is the art of zazen" (quoted in Dumoulin, 1969, p. 161).

Bonpu ("ordinary") zazen is the first level of Zen sitting. It is the zazen of the ordinary person who wants to improve his health, develop himself, and achieve some inner peace. I consider it the basic therapeutic device of Zen. Bonpu zazen may be practiced according to the description of Dogen we have quoted, with some simplifications for the beginner.

First, the lotus-sitting position may be preferred, which is what Dogen describes, but is not essential. Zazen may be practiced in a straight-backed chair (as described in the fourth chapter, on Seiza) or while walking or lying down. The important consideration is assuming a stable position that will neither require your attention to maintain nor permit you to fall asleep. After one learns how to go about it, bonpu sitting can even be practiced effectively while riding on a bus or train.

Outside distractions should be minimized, but monotonous traffic sounds, for example, are endurable. Beginners may start with ten- to thirty-minute periods twice a day (Sato, 1961).

In bonpu sitting the person concentrates on his breathing, mentally counting each breath. There are various styles of bonpu sitting, and different masters have different preferences. One can count each inhalation and exhalation up to ten, then start over; one can count only exhalations; one can extend the exhalations and the internal count, as oooooone, twooooo, threeeee, and so forth.

For the beginner, the purpose of counting is to help him maintain his mental concentration in the presence of various drifting thoughts. In Kapleau we read, "Let random thoughts arise and vanish as they will, do not dally with them and do not try to expel them, but merely concentrate all your energy on counting" (Kapleau, 1965, p. 33). With practice the intrusive thoughts decline, but some meditators keep a notebook and pad at their side to jot down the most important ideas that arise so that they can be considered at leisure later. The key to success here is to avoid struggling with one's own mind, a process that only distracts from meditation. Recognize the intrusion and let it pass through as you return to the counting.

At the International Congress for Psychosomatic Medicine and Hypnosis in 1967, Kasamatsu and Hirai reported on their brain wave research during the meditation of forty-eight Zen priests and disciples (Hirai, 1975). Within fifty seconds of beginning meditation alpha waves appeared, then increased. These wave patterns indicate a state of mental relaxation; they might have been the same if the Zen meditators were drowsing. But they were not drowsing, as the next experiment showed. Fairly loud clicks were repeated at intervals for a total of twenty times in the ears of each subject. The clicks have a predictable effect on a drowsing person. They disrupt his drowsiness, reducing the number of alpha waves for quite awhile; but after he has heard several of the clicks their effect diminishes. It is as if the drowsing person's mind tells him, "Don't be bothered now; it's only another of those clicks—we'll ignore them." But the response of the Zen priests to the clicks was quite different. When the clicks began, the alpha waves diminished momentarily, but they quickly returned (three to five seconds later). Each time a click sounded, even on the twentieth time, the response was the same. It was as if the Zen meditator were alert to the incoming stimulus of each moment; it rippled through his awareness, and he returned to his meditative state.

As skill develops in concentration, counting may be dispensed with and visualizing one's breathing may be substituted. The client pictures the air coming in through the nose, passing into the expanding abdomen, and going back out again. The sinuous course can be imagined in detail.

Concentration on breathing seems to have two major purposes. First, the mind is gradually stilled. Herrigel was studying Zen archery when he wrote the following: "It took considerable time before I succeeded in doing what the Master wanted. But—I succeeded. I learned to lose myself so effortlessly in the breathing that I sometimes had the feeling that I myself was not breathing but—strange as this may sound—being breathed" (Herrigel, 1971, p. 40).

Second, a link is reinstituted between the conscious mind and a basic physiological function. "To be conscious is characteristic of the human mind as distinguished from the animal mind. But when the mind becomes conscious of its doings, it ceases to be instinctual and its commands are colored with calculations and deliberations—which means that the connection between itself and the limbs is no longer direct" (Suzuki, 1959, p. 110). Zazen aims at reestablishing that connection with resultant spontaneity and naturalness.

Wienpahl stated it this way: "How do you get beyond ideas (save in sleep and running, for example) except by something like zazen, the practice of being without ideas? As such it can be done in any position. Sitting and breathing in a certain manner may just help it, or be introductory to it. However, customary ways of sitting help to induce old habits; of thinking, for example" (Wienpahl, 1970, p. 57).

Before we leave bonpu zazen, I should like to point out experiences some westerners share that I believe are useful in understanding the unity of consciousness and action promoted by this form of Zen sitting. The skillful typist cannot take time to decide which key to press. The words flow through the mind and are transferred to the keyboard. The basketball player who concentrates too carefully on the game plan or on what needs to be done will miss the quick pass, the open shot at the basket. The golfer who allows worries or pressure to interfere with the natural swing of his club is in trouble. The driver suddenly discovers he is near his turnoff but cannot remember traveling the past five or ten miles. These are all experiences linking awareness and action. Zazen aims at harmonizing that link.

Zen Practice: Enlightenment

In this section I shall expand the notion of neurotic to include everyone, and the notion of therapy to include an enlightenment experience. There is a sense in which all zazen, even forms other than bonpu zazen, are therapy. From the Buddhist perspective, and in the Buddha's words, "All worldlings are insane." We simply don't realize that the permanence we ascribe to this world is evanescent. It isn't realistic to live as if we expect the world as it is at this moment to continue indefinitely.

Erich Fromm observed that "These new 'patients' come to the psychoanalyst without knowing what they really suffer from. They complain about being depressed, having insomnia, being unhappy in their marriages, not enjoying their work, and any number of similar troubles. They usually believe that this or that particular symptom is their problem and that if they could get rid of this particular trouble they would be well. However, these patients usually do not see that their problem is not that of depression, of insomnia, of their marriage, or of their jobs. These various complaints are only the conscious form in which our culture permits them to express something which lies much deeper, and which is common to the various people who consciously believe that they suffer from this or that particular symptom. The common suffering is the alienation from oneself, from one's fellow man, and from nature; the awareness that life runs out of one's hand like sand, and that one will die without having lived; that one lives in the midst of plenty and yet is joyless" (Suzuki et al., 1963, pp. 85–86).

We hide from our impotence and aloneness in shelters of conformity, routine, dependency; in the limited cellars of sex, power, and money; in the illusion that tomorrow will not bring pain, suffering, aging, and death.

Zen, like any religion, proclaims answers to these existential issues. There are countless books about Zen's proposed solution. I wouldn't presume to rewrite them. I do believe, however, that Zen's strategy for facing these human dilemmas is not unlike that of Morita therapy. That is why I began and ended the descriptions of these quiet therapies with Morita therapy and Zen, respectively.

Wienpahl learned from his Zen roshi that "It is not enjoying the sun or the rain when they are there. Or avoiding them. It is taking the days as they come. And they come anyhow. All the 'this is good' or 'this is bad' and the fretting are coming out of you. In this way one sees that they are illusions" (Wienpahl, 1970, p. 120).

VII
Conclusion

WE TEND TO DESCRIBE OURSELVES in terms of absolutes. Am I weak or strong? Am I sad or joyful? A good person or a bad person? But when I look within myself, when I examine my experience carefully, I find a condition much too complex to be put into words. I am both weak and strong in various mixtures in various situations at various times. Sadness and joy chase each other around my psyche, blending, supplementing, fleeing altogether. I am good and bad from various perspectives with similarly complex shifts and combinations.

It is the change or flux that is real. It is the complexity that is real. The simple statements that I am sad or strong or good are abstractions from the "complicated changingness" that is me. So what? Well, any therapy that fails to take into account this changeable complexity in my experience, any therapy that treats me as a neurotic person or tries to get rid of my anxiety or fear is treating not me but an abstraction of me. I am no more a constant neurotic than I am steadily good or happy. My anxieties, self-doubts, and fears are no more constant than my strengths or my joys.

How can a therapy treat flux? We need something to focus on as a target of change, something to deal with directly, don't we? Apparently not. The therapies discussed in this book seem to treat the flux, the flow of awareness directly. Since that flow is all we ever experience, is what we *are* in a very basic way, it seems appropriate to focus therapeutic intervention there.

The goal of these therapies seems to be a kind of focusing and regulation of this flow of consciousness. In shadan the flow is slowed down, then gradually restarted with minor mental tasks. In naikan it is focused topically on the past, but the pace also slows somewhat over the period of meditation. In Morita therapy it is allowed to flow unhindered during bed rest, then reigned in and focused on tasks and purposes thereafter. In seiza and Zen it is directed inward to focus on breathing, counting, or other mental exercises. Overall, the implication seems to be that the uneasy mind is misfocused and mispaced. Let us look at these two misfunctions.

The misfocused mind is overly self-focused, selfish. The strategy of therapy, then, is to refocus attention away from the everyday self-consciousness. Therapy can seek to flood awareness with self, as in Zen and seiza and Morita therapy's isolated bed rest, to induce a breakthrough to a deeper self (not subconscious but superconscious) or perhaps a surfeit of self-focus. Another tactic is to flood awareness with a negative self-consciousness, as in naikan; the result is a need to serve others and sacrifice the previously ungrateful, unaware self. The third tactic is to assign tasks that pull attention away from the self, as is done in the assigned mental work of shadan and the task focus of Morita therapy.

The functioning of the disturbed person's mind has also been mispaced. Either it has been unchecked, fleeing from topic to topic to escape distressing thoughts and feelings, or it becomes stuck on some obsessive rumination or in some compulsive ritual. All of the quiet therapies reflect this pacing of the flow of thought by isolating the client, reducing the stimulus input available to his senses, and encouraging him to be physically still. The result is a slowing of thought processes and, it is believed, a deepening of them as well.

Talking may be used to reveal oneself to oneself and to others. But perhaps it is used more often to disguise and conceal

our inner states. These therapies discourage the use of talk as
an escape for the client. When speaking is permitted at all, it
is allowed only in circumscribed situations, often with the
purpose of checking on the client's progress (as in the periodic interviews of naikan and the interviews with the roshi in
some forms of Zen training). Even then it is said that a skilled
therapist can determine the client's inner state merely by not-
ing the condition of his eyes. Words are not necessary. Complete silence is requested at one Moritist hospital, and talking
is limited in the others.

A premise underlying these simple therapeutic strategies is
the fundamental Buddhist one that man is essentially good,
in need only of education to achieve a better state of mind.
Quiet isolation brings about the opportunity for our natural
inner strength to lead us toward a more enlightened understanding of ourselves. But the inner strength needs some guidance to work most effectively.

On Happiness

Let us think about happiness for a few moments. Americans
seem to be obsessed with happiness. Even the United States
Constitution guarantees American citizens the right to pursue this elusive state. Amusement parks promise us the gid-
dier forms of happiness—thrills, excitement. Movies and
television offer us more prosaic "enjoyment." Our religious
establishments display a presumably deeper form of happiness, joy. Drugs offer a high. Breath mints tout zing. Profes-
sors are prodded to help students enjoy their education. Mod-
els smile; politicians grin and wave; announcers fade from
view with lips in frozen professional curls.

Our obsession with happiness struck home deepest for me
as I observed people try to deal with others' depressions. The
underlying premise was almost universally that the depressed
person ought not to be sad, that the natural state for human
beings should be one of happiness. The techniques by which
others attempted to pull these sad people out of their misery

were often joking or kidding, trying to make them smile, to feel better.

Of course no one believes we can stay gloriously happy twenty-four hours a day, yet life for many Americans (and many modern-day Japanese) seems often to be measured in terms of its high points and its overall satisfaction. But is this strategy for dealing with life reasonable or even desirable? Let's see what the quiet therapies have to say about admitting all of life into our game plan of existence.

On Acceptance

A Buddhist principle that permeates all of these therapies may be described briefly as the acceptance of inevitable reality. Suffering, in particular, is an integral part of life. When suffering occurs (because of illness, aging, loss, and so forth), any attempt to deny or displace the inner pain only intensifies it.

In these therapies the client must accept his immediate condition—the boredom and discomfort and disillusionment at first, the stray thoughts that intrude on his meditation, the reality of his distress. Such is his life now. In a small way, acceptance of his life during therapy is paradigmatic of the acceptance that must come throughout his life.

Acceptance is not passive resignation. Giving up is inconsistent with entering therapy to improve one's state of mind. One does what one can. On the other hand, as one Moritist said, there is no sense in trying to shovel away our shadows.

The Buddhist idea of acceptance is not essentially different from the Christian concept of "God's will be done." Both concepts are quite effective in some circumstances, freeing the mind from obsessively trying to change what cannot be changed, allowing the mind to turn to new issues and problems.

The prayer of Alcoholics Anonymous includes not only the admonition to change what can be changed but also to accept what cannot be changed. Human life wisdom crops up in various guises but usually in more than one place and at more than one time. Again, elements of these Eastern life principles are not so unfamiliar after all when appropriate parallel illustrations are pointed out.

The result of acceptance is not only freedom from being stuck on "what-ought-to-be-but-isn't" or "what-might-have-been-but-wasn't"; it also opens up the opportunity to relish all of life. No longer are there high points interspersed by long periods of just getting by. The sadness, joy, hope, fear, loneliness, passion, and despair of each moment become acceptable title pages to the constantly changing monograph of my life. No experience needs to be hidden away in a footnote or appendix. What is now *is*.

On Accommodation to Human Frailty

Each therapy described in this book makes some allowance for the imperfection of the human body. Naikan allows the client to sit in any position that is comfortable for him. The only restriction is that he may not lie down for fear of drowsiness. Seiza allows the client to raise himself as necessary from a sitting position in which his buttocks are resting on his heels to a kneeling position so that circulation can return to his lower extremities. Shadan therapy and the isolated bed rest of Morita therapy permit the client to lie in any comfortable reclining position. Zen sitting is interspersed by periods of meditation while walking and ritual blows to the shoulders to relieve muscle strain and drowsiness.

Far from ignoring the body or punishing it with unremitting harsh and ascetic discipline, these therapies recognize the potential for distracting attention that physical pain holds. Some relief is offered to keep the client in therapy and allow him to participate in it fully.

We find no artificial separation of the mind and body here. Perhaps shadan's theoretical uniting of the two is most extreme, but each of these therapies works mind and body together in parallel fashion to achieve its ends. Stilling mind and body, feeding mind and body, exercising mind and body, disciplining mind and body, purifying mind and body, and so forth—the parallels are common. Also, in each form of therapy there is recognition that the psychological progress of the client is reflected in his body. His eyes, his facial expression, his posture, his walk tell the therapist where the client is on his path to maturity.

On Therapy as Resocialization

The theme of resocialization, that is, becoming a social child and socially growing up again, can be seen most clearly in naikan, but it is certainly present in the other quiet therapies as well.

As we have seen, one basic reason for naikan's effectiveness is the primary restructuring of the client's view of his past that takes place during naikan therapy. He relives his childhood in memory, attending to details he hadn't emphasized before and ignoring or dismissing others he had previously considered dominant. The desired result is a re-formed, mature adult who is more loving and giving.

Although the procedures may require an adult's self-discipline and attention span, all of the therapies regress the client into a childlike *social* state. The bed rest of the shadan and Morita therapies puts the client in a helpless, dependent condition, simplifying his world into one much like that of a baby. The quiet immobility of all meditative therapies is closer to the condition of infancy than to any other human stage of development except, perhaps, the stage of very old age and the approach of death.

Therapists are parental, wise, and experienced. Fellow clients are like brothers and sisters. The family theme of Morita therapy is worked out in detail in another book, *Morita Psychotherapy* (Reynolds, 1976), but the threads for a familylike resocialization setting can be found in each of these therapies. For that matter, familylike orientation permeates much of Japanese culture, even the business world.

The point is that when one considers long-term distress (neurosis) to be a result of an inadequate view of reality and educational training (therapy) to be the means to achieve resolution to this distress, the model of educational training within the family (socialization) offers a ready framework for organizing the therapeutic effort.

Some side effects of this return to a sort of childhood include temporary relief from everyday responsibilities (with some reduction of anxiety) and increased influenceability and suggestibility (giving the therapist a better psychological foothold).

Key Days in Therapy

Timing is fundamental to the success of any therapy. Again and again in reading accounts of these quiet therapies my attention was drawn to the fourth and fifth days of treatment. In Morita's isolated bed rest, in naikan, in shadan, and in the *sesshin* (a concentrated period) of zazen—in each of the quiet therapies that advises intensive therapy over a week or so, the fourth and fifth days are frequently believed to be critical.

It is during this two-day span that the client is likely to reach some peak experience. Until then he has been buffeted by doubts and distractions. Usually the therapist has warned him that initially he will question the usefulness of the practice. He may want to leave the setting. His mind will wander. The therapist asks him to follow instructions and wait out the week. He need not believe that his effort will produce fruit; he is requested only to do as he is told.

But by the time this critical period has been reached the simple life routine has been assimilated. The inner focus has deepened and strengthened. Outer stimuli, so important as inhibitors of the inner focus, have been reduced by the simple setting, the still posture, and the closed or semiclosed eyes.

Why it should take four or five days for many clients to reach this state of inner awareness I do not know. It is a comment about the hold our externally directed senses and thought processes have on our awareness. At any rate, in these key days some peak experience is likely to occur. Of course, the experience varies from client to client. Often it involves a kind of giving up of self or some part of the self that the client previously considered important. There may be a restructuring of the client's view of himself and his world. There is frequently a powerful emotional component. Tears, a change in the tone of the voice, elation, joy, peace, anguish, despair, and complex combinations of these and other feelings and behaviors are common.

This shake-up is often followed by a reaction to the intensity of the experience and the inactivity that preceded it. The client may feel bored and restricted. He may strongly desire to leave the setting, to work, to make restitution to those he has wronged, to share his insights with others.

The wise therapist uses this urge for activity, too, in teaching the lessons of acceptance and of self-awareness. The client is encouraged to work harder in the few remaining days to deepen his understanding of himself.

This cycle of boredom and doubt, gradually deepening inner focus, peak experience, increasing boredom, and desire for activity occurs again and again in the literature and in the verbal accounts of patients; and, as has been stressed, it occurs frequently within the same one-week time frame. I have experienced it twice while undergoing Moritist isolated bed rest and naikan therapy as part of my research in Japan. Despite our individual and cultural variations, we human beings are basically not so different after all.

Concluding Thoughts

In this final section some readers may expect me to draw together the material from these five meditative therapies and to fit their effects into some Western scientific theoretical scheme. I am not certain I can do the latter; I am doubtful that we have a schema that makes adequate predictive and explanatory sense of what appears to happen in the minds and lives of the patients of the quiet therapies.

Furthermore, the reader will find no systematic comparison of Japanese therapies with Western modes of treatment. I have undertaken that exercise in *Morita Psychotherapy* (Reynolds, 1976). In any case, there is a sense in which such a comparison would be less useful than might be expected. With few, minor exceptions, Western psychotherapy can be characterized as verbal exchanges aimed at elimination of symptoms. The Japanese therapies are marked by significant, long periods of silence aimed at acceptance, incorporation, and transcendence of symptoms. My symptoms *are* me. They are not an external, isolated problem of mine—so these therapists argue. This book has aimed at presenting their case in terms familiar and recognizable to readers from a Western cultural background.

The five quiet therapies are deeply rooted in Eastern ways of thinking and behaving. Some of them have borrowed Western techniques and rationales, yet all remain fundamentally Asian in outlook. Have they any relevance to Western peoples? Can they provide partial or complete solutions to worldwide problems of dissatisfaction, dis-ease, and unrest? Such questions cannot be answered simply with thinking, pen, and ink. They require experience; that is, they require testing. Perhaps we cannot afford to delay their testing much longer.

At any rate, before we can offer them a trial we must reach some understanding of their techniques and their intent. We must find that these therapies' views of man and suffering make sense in terms of our own experience; otherwise, there is no reason to pursue an evaluation of them in practice. Whether or not your experience resonates to the chords of these ideas I do not know. But reading this book is a step.

Appendix:
On Boredom, Brain Waves,
and Bliss

WESTERN PSYCHOLOGY has taken a recent interest in some of the processes that may be operating during these quiet therapies. Smith (1976) offers a readable brief review article on the therapeutic effectiveness of isolation and its accompanying boredom. He notes that Suedfeld (1975) found sensory deprivation to have therapeutic value in treating smoking addiction and phobias.

Isolation brings on increased awareness of body sensations. It disrupts ordinary patterns of cognition, allowing the patient to begin to respond to new cues, to consider and experience new possibilities for action. The isolation intensifies the impact and amplifies the value of social reinforcement. My estimation of you and your advice is related to how much I need human contact at any given time.

But Suedfeld pointed out that "the effects of sensory deprivation are more psychological than physiological" (quoted in Smith, 1976, p. 50). That is an important comment. Until now, it is on the psychological level of description and analysis that both Western and Eastern attempts to reach an understanding of these phenomena make the most sense to me. Physiological studies are inconclusive despite their appeal to the reductionist bias of the West.

Grossberg (1972) has written an excellent critical review article attacking the overextension of brain wave feedback explanations for changes in psychological events and states. It is tempting to try to tie the mental state of relaxed alertness to measurable brain potentials such as alpha waves, to tie subjective experience to objective physiologic electrical output. Yet so many variables influence alpha wave density that the investigators cited by Grossberg can conclude that there is no simple direct relationship between alpha rhythms and any feeling state.

Grossberg argues that a person's report of what is happening in his psyche is so strongly influenced by situational and personal-historical factors that no simple biological or physiological account of emotion will ever satisfactorily explain his psychological state.

There is no reason to reject outright the systematically accumulated self-reports of the thousands of patients who have experienced profound psychological change while engaged in these quiet therapies. Their introspective reports, along with the observations of their therapists and accounts written by outside observers, give us important clues to psychological mechanisms working within the human mind. At this point we have not progressed much beyond the level of description. The patient does X and Y and quite often he experiences Z_1 and does Z_2. The explanations offered for the experience and the behavior are, in my opinion, not particularly convincing thus far, whether they are Eastern or Western. However, the reality of the changes of outlook and behaviors cannot be denied.

In an article that remains on the descriptive and experiential level, Furlong (1976) reports on the "flow" experience. The concept of flow came from the accounts of surgeons, composers, chess players, painters, modern dancers, baseball players, and others who found that there were periods in their lives when they were fully involved in an endeavor, acting spontaneously yet in full control, attending with sharp awareness, sensing a kind of merging of themselves and their activity. This flow provides the most rewarding element of their profession. It offers them a special joy in living.

Csikszentmihalyi (1976) believes that this flow is possible in any activity and that it can be experienced by all of us a good deal of the time. I agree. And so do the quiet therapists.

Afterword

DAVID REYNOLDS HAS WRITTEN a very perceptive and illuminating book on forms of psychotherapy now appearing in modern Japan. I have been asked to create some conceptual bridges between these indigenous developments and contemporary concerns in Western psychology and, at the same time, to relate these very Japanese forms of therapy to other features of Japanese culture.

In looking at the quiet therapies I find they stimulate in me two questions. The first arises when one observes that among those seeking therapeutic intervention in Japan it is quite evident that psychoanalytic therapy has gained very few subjects, in contrast to what has been occurring in Western Europe and the United States. This is so despite the ability of contemporary Japanese to afford its cost. Why is psychoanalysis so lacking in popularity when Japanese have been so indiscriminate in sampling other intellectual and artistic products of Western culture and in developing native Japanese performers?

This question leads to another. Can we somehow relate the seeming efficacy in an appreciable number of cases of the quiet therapies to patterns of cultural continuity still embedded in Japanese family life? Are there still to be observed peculiarities of Japanese thought patterns, structuring of emotions, and perception of interpersonal relationships that can help us explain why Japanese respond to certain forms of therapeutic intervention and not to others?

Culturally Determined Patterns of Thought and Concepts of Psychotherapy

To approach the second question first, it may well be that American specialists in psychotherapy will find Reynolds' approach to the quiet therapies disquieting. He does not immediately classify, and basic questions may arise in the mind of the specialist. For example, what is the underlying causal pattern of the malaise experienced by the Japanese patients? What are the early experiences contributing to these peculiar forms of psychological difficulty? How and why does psychotherapy work? What are the statistics of cure? Reynolds' approach makes no serious attempt to answer such questions. It offers no psychodynamic explanations, no analysis of problems in Japanese socialization. In fact, he really makes no attempt to use the concept of causality, nor does he seriously attempt to justify therapeutic procedures by citing objective statistics. In his description of these therapies he points out instead that Morita therapy or naikan therapy does not in itself seek to explain human psychology in any depth, nor does it seek to justify its practice by statistical or other means related to an exposition of relative efficacy. Rather, the major concern is with behavior and change in performance. The individual going into one of these therapies does not need elaborate explanatory principles as a means of approach to his malaise. What he seeks is not an explanation of his illness but a renewed capacity to perform well in what he expects of himself. Again, the "ego" is not the concern, nor is the development of self-consciousness the instrumental purpose of the therapy. On the contrary, excessive self-consciousness in itself may be a problem to be ameliorated.

What is delightful about this book is that Reynolds seeks to instruct us in the meaning of the quiet therapies simply by participation. It is through his own experience that he seeks to communicate to us. He wants us to share, insofar as it is possible, in the experiencing of the therapies rather than in a discussion of the differences between East and West or of why and how therapeutic procedures work. The latter attempt would have produced a far different volume. Therefore the reader is requested to leave go his own need for explanation and to follow Reynolds' guidance into the world of the quiet therapies.

What Reynolds is doing is challenging us to give up our culturally developed modes of thinking about therapy and approach the subject as far as possible in the way the Japanese themselves approach it. I shall not attempt to do here what Reynolds has not done, but what I will discuss briefly is the cultural differences to be noted between Japan and our own tradition in the socialization of cognitive processes.

In our formal education we are brought up in a type of thinking in which analysis dominates. That is to say, we learn about things contrastively. We learn to keep our ideas consistent by delineating categories. Starting with the concrete, our classifications become more and more abstract. Whether we directly recognize it or not, we more or less all practice an Aristotelian form of logic. Levi-Strauss, in his *Structural Anthropology*, seeks to impose this type of thinking upon all mankind. He can be seriously questioned for this presumption. Similarly, Mary Douglas, one of the foremost British anthropologists today, in her analysis of concepts such as "purity" as they are experienced cross-culturally, implicitly falls back on her own Judeo-Christian mode of analysis as a means of explanation. She suggests that conceptual anomaly is the ultimate contamination. Indeed, it is hard for those of us brought up in this tradition to leave go of it sufficiently to attempt forms of thought that flow more spontaneously in channels used in a totally different cultural tradition.

In our tradition conscious control is obtained by constraining our thought into linear progressions that create a sense of causality. Whereas Western thought in its highest form has been analytic, the Japanese have sought to develop the syncretic—the visual-spacial rather than the verbal-sequential—mode of thought. Western religious thought has not been without its use of the visual. It is Kenneth Clark who, for me, defined the great revolution of the Reformation in Western thought by pointing out how the Reformation in northern Europe went from religious representation in ritual and in image to a Judaic concern with the word itself. In returning to the verbal message of the Bible, the northern Reformation did away with the visual, and emotionally charged, reaffirmations of collective ritual. Visual display and personal participation in ritual were replaced by a greater attention to the word of God. The Thomistic revival of orthodox Catholicism responded to this revolution with a reapplication of Aristotilean logic to religious dogma.

Japanese thought has not developed any tradition of Aristotilean syllogism. In religion it has shown little regard for logic and nowhere can one find any attempt at a formal proof of the existence of God. Retaining the metaphor as the principal mode of understanding, Japanese see relationships more readily in a poetic dimension. They remain capable of communicating with one another through allusion, so that individuals recognize what is being said by metaphorical implication. Feelings and nuances of feeling are more important in this type of expression than analytic concern with sequential causality. This difference in thought has led in its extremity, for example, to the derogation of the Shinto faith by Western observers as "not even a religion," because it remains so maddeningly inchoate. Thoughts or concepts interpenetrate one another. There is no attempt at definition of singularity as distinct from plurality. The concept of deity itself is at times so amorphous that it cannot be subjected to any consistent exposition. How can you have a recognized religion without systematic dogma? How can you have a religion in which there is no conflict perceived between itself and practices of other faiths? How can you have a religion without any conscious sense of heterodoxy or heresy? Throughout the Japanese tradition one finds that there has never been any serious worry about conceptual inconsistencies in religious thought.

The one area of precise categorization implicit in the Japanese language is that of social hierarchy. Excruciating tension is aroused in Japanese in respect to differential status, and therefore minute attention is paid in language forms to appropriate levels of deference and politeness. But this type of careful consideration never becomes a concern for clarity as such. Orderly exposition of thought is not traditionally regarded as an exemplary virtue, nor are diffuseness and obfuscation seen as a contrary vice.

This contrast I am depicting should help prepare one to appreciate the type of thought found functional and fundamental in Zen, where attempts to lose oneself in abstraction are discouraged and no attempt is made to control either the self or nature through an application of systematic thought. One does not seek to control the world through thought. Rather, one seeks to gain control of oneself by dispensing with dissonant considerations that lead one astray.

Reynolds suggests that an operational or functional definition of "cookie" would be its recipe whereas a dictionary definition of cookie would be some form of categorization or abstraction. In our Western evaluation of intelligence we reward abstraction as a higher form of thought. For example, when one grades answers on a subtest of a Wechsler intelligence scale, two points are given for spontaneous answers to "similarities" defined on an abstract basis; only one point is given for a functional description of similarities between objects. We reward abstraction because Western culture, in its attempt to control nature, has found it extremely useful. In Western forms of education we have indeed nurtured a maturation of cognitive controls that order the external world through the manipulation of abstract thought.

But this attention to external control is only one possible mode in which "primary process thinking" is socialized. A concern with control is also found in "magical" thought; and psychoanalytic considerations of primary process thinking examine how magical thought uses words as parts of objects—control of words allows us to control the objects. It is only with a certain kind of maturation that these primitive, prelogical forms of thought become harnessed and trained toward objective and scientific concerns with causality.

We might notice that, at the same time that magical, prelogical modes of thought are developing, other mental mechanisms are also developing around concerns with synthesis, not analysis. The early ego develops a capacity to comprehend patterns of similarity in the world as well as patterns of difference that separate objects. These syncretic forms of early thought are nurtured in cultures that give priority to the development of a sense of belonging and participation. What one finds, therefore, is that whereas some cultures nurture control over analytic modes of cognitive development, other cultures are more concerned with the syncretic and the metaphoric. These two modes can both be brought to forms of maturation that transcend their primitive origins in the early primary process thinking.

No follower of Zen would ever arrive at Einstein's formula for relativity. The physics that Einstein developed allows us now, however, to gain some grasp of a very complex universe that is not linear in functioning. Yet we have reached this conceptualization of such a universe by exercising precise control over thought arranged in linear patterns. We have found in the Western tradition the ultimate utility of abstraction. But there is a danger there, because as human beings we sometimes believe we are experiencing abstractions when indeed we are experiencing our existence through our concrete feelings. We can create a recipe for making cookies and communicate it, but the proof of the cookie is in the eating. Abstractions about cookies will never reveal to us the taste of the experience. Again, this is the essential experiential argument of Zen in its approach to life. What Reynolds is trying to have us do is taste the cookie. He is not trying to tell us why or how we are tasting it, or whether, indeed, the experience itself will be the same for those brought up on a different cuisine. The experience of the cookie could conceivably be distasteful if our socialization has led us to find its particular taste unpleasant.

The experience of the quiet therapies is not for everyone. There are some underlying presumptions in them which assume a certain innate human goodness: quiet isolation brings about an opportunity for one's positive inner nature to manifest and spontaneously direct itself, perhaps, toward greater enlightenment. The quiet therapies promote a form of experiential understanding that allows consciousness to flow in a constructive direction. One can readily see that the type of presumption that underlies these therapies may not be universally shared and that the therapies may have certain limitations in respect to those who can benefit from their practice. Indeed, some may fear that in isolation their thoughts will lead them in a negative direction. They may so fear their impulses that to sit quietly may be an intolerable hazard.

As is true for most forms of therapy, the quiet therapies are not universally applicable; they are efficacious within a cultural context. There are traditions within Japanese culture called upon in therapeutic practice that may seem strange to Americans. There is, for example, the use of the diary in Morita therapy, drawing upon a custom very widespread in Japan where individuals are used to recording their thoughts in some form of a daily journal. In fact, it is sometimes easier for individuals to write down their thoughts than to relate them directly to another person. There are occasions in Japan when people will make their diaries available but will never communicate directly, verbally, about their experiences. The diary is used not only to communicate with oneself, but sometimes to communicate with others.

Can the quiet therapies find appeal among Americans? We note in bookstores around the universities today more volumes dealing with the occult or with non-Western religious traditions than with either modern psychology or traditional Christianity. This interest in the nonrational is symptomatic of a search for the syncretic, the novel, the strange, the non-Western. There is dissatisfaction with an overemphasis on reason and instrumental individual goals. There is also a sense that American society is anomic, that it produces alienation in its youth, that its individualistic emphasis has been at the expense of developing capacities for belonging and participation. The seeking that we witness among a younger generation of Americans comes out of a deep sense of revolt against family insufficiency as well as a revolt against cognitive discipline. Can Eastern philosophy or Eastern wisdom supply more satisfactory answers?

The quiet therapies have two presumptions that may not satisfy young Americans caught in generational conflict. First, they require some form of self-discipline. Second, they reconcile the individual to the legitimate functioning of parents. Moreover, there is a profound understanding of a human need to express gratitude. What is deeply hurtful when one is overcome by strong feelings of resentment is one's incapacity to release any sentiment of gratitude toward some other being. Without attempting to understand the complexity of this emotion or its origin in early infantile experience, let us say that in many forms taken by Japanese psychotherapy there is an emphasis on how to direct or give reason for a sense of gratitude toward one's parents. As it is precisely the parents who are being rejected by many young Americans seeking new forms of religious adherence or therapeutic relief, I would think that these therapies would have appeal only in very limited cases, given the contemporary American social atmosphere.

I remember witnessing in Tokyo, at the large temple complex of Risshō Kōseikai (a so-called new religion although it claims direct lineage from early Buddhism), a "group therapy" session held for housewives. In the session I attended these modern housewives were being reconciled by a group leader to the idea that Japanese men are often childlike—hence, it should not be surprising that they sometimes "play around" with other women. I found that this organization, like several others of the new religions that are so popular in contemporary Japan, actually hires professional psychologists as advisors or consultants to help in guidance programs. These sects are aware of Western social science and its concepts of group dynamics and like to consider themselves modern and "international"; yet their programs are directed for the most part toward reconciling the individual to occupational and traditional family roles. They do not set forth a goal of "self-actualization" or personal transformation, nor do they seek to develop a religious fellowship that might take the individual away from the family as the central value through which emotional fulfillment is to be found. Winifred Dahl, in a yet-to-be-published study of religious conversion experiences among Japanese Americans, illustrates significant differences in family orientation between those joining a Christian church, with its emphasis on a new spiritual brotherhood external to the primary family, and those joining an American branch of a Japanese new religion. In the latter case there is a redirection of positive feelings toward parental figures, especially the mother.

In the Christian tradition, a corresponding sense of love and gratitude is stimulated through the image of the sacrificial Christ. This power-image has been a revolutionary social force for almost two thousand years, supplanting the deities of house and lineage of the Roman family tradition and then the native deities of pagan Europe. It has fostered the development of universalist principles of morality transcending family roles and obligations and has afforded psychological leverage against not only the absolute family but the absolute state as well. The Christian Church, whatever its vicissitudes in the exercise of temporal power, has maintained for itself a monopoly in the realm of the sacred and has promised its adherents, through its millenarian myth, a personal survival unrelated to family role or identity. As a result, Western forms of religion, and of psychotherapy as well, implicitly convey ideals of personal maturation that are individualistic, even antifamilial. The individual soul, which is promised a direct personal relationship with deity, is conceived of as eternally separate from others.

If we turn to Japan and examine the history of Buddhism as another universalist religious philosophy which in some respects is concerned with individual salvation, we find that it never superceded the family as a force in shaping social morality. Although Buddhist reformers of the twelfth and thirteenth centuries developed powerful social messages, Buddhism never finally replaced the communal folk beliefs of Shinto, on the one hand, or the Confucian moral principles that supported the legitimacy of family and state, on the other. Moreover, the promise of nirvana in Buddhist thought is not one in which the individual entity will continue, but rather one in which it will mercifully disappear. In Buddhism the self is an illusion, and the sense of separateness so painfully a part of becoming human is transitory, in that it will not persist through all eternity but, as promised, will find release in oblivion.

Consider, too, the encompassing womblike vagueness of Shinto thought, in which the concept of *kami* is plural as well as singular. The war dead that hover about the Yasukumi Jinja, a shrine commemorating those lost in battle, are indefinitely referred to as "spirit." Thus, becoming kami is not a promise of continuity of personality or of continued separateness. Kami, as part of the flow of life called the Yamato Race, partake of the sacred without maintaining distinctive individuality.

Nor does Confucianism have a place for individualistic concepts of the person. There are no individuals as such—only family members whose roles change through the life cycle. At no time is the person regarded as separate from his family and social roles, and maturation is a deepening of understanding of one's place in a system, that is, in a social unit which is, again, part of yet a larger social unit. One's ultimate duty, as well as one's ultimate psychological security, is to be found in family or group continuity, not in the continuity of the self.

Given this divergence between Christian and Far Eastern religious traditions, it should not be surprising that modernization through industrial technology and social organization does not, in different cultures, inevitably result in the same ways of defining social and psychological problems. Cultures do become secular, but the secular concepts they evolve, especially in dealing with emotions, are not always similar cross-culturally.

The concept of psychotherapy, whether in the United States or in Japan, is a secular one, supplanting more religious ones that offer solace for human malaise. Approaches to psychotherapy therefore supposedly grow out of attempts to apply a science of psychology to human problems. But whatever the cognitive universalization resulting from familiarity with science and scientific methods, the subjective experiencing of emotions remains more culture-bound. Perceptions and interpretations of feelings remain stubbornly attuned to the socialization derived from a cultural tradition that still influences heavily the primary experiences of infancy and childhood.

Consider the fact that Western social science itself is somewhat culture-bound. It is so "rationalistic" and individualistic in some of its theories that it tends to see all human action as based on utilitarian self-interest. Some theorists even presume that a materialist economic determinism can explain all social history. Such rational theories of human motivation, however, cannot explain the flow of events in a "modern" Japan. Nor do they explain the events now occurring in "modern" Islamic states.

In the West psychoanalytic theory is sometimes rejected because it suggests behavior is irrationally motivated. When Western intellectuals reject psychoanalysis, it is often because it suggests too strongly to them that they are not as rationally or instrumentally motivated as they would like to consider themselves to be. They are not in control of their own thought processes as much as they would like to be. They cannot bend the flow of history to their own rational purpose. Western social theory is uneasy about what some sociologists refer to as "primordial feelings," which cause individuals in modern as well as premodern societies to go against what would be their ultimate instrumental advantage.

As we shall presently see, the Japanese continue to reject psychoanalytic theories not because they are about an irrational unconscious per se, but because delving into this unconscious threatens family cohesion. Tensions experienced through a conflict of occupational expectations or family role versus disruptive private feelings are most frequently resolved in Japan by directing the individual back toward the family. The goals of attempts to alleviate psychiatric problems are therefore defined in terms of family or occupational integration.

Psychotherapy:
The Experience of Gratitude and the Sense of Guilt

The reason that Japanese do not seek personal resolution of psychiatric problems through depth therapies such as psychoanalysis is not simply because Japanese reject scientific psychology on an intellectual level. One must therefore ask, what in psychoanalysis makes it *emotionally* impossible for Japanese? Looked at in context, the growth of psychoanalysis in the West cannot be separated from the cultural tradition that gave it birth. Psychoanalysis has, as its basic premise, the autonomy of the individual. Autonomy is an awesome concept. It can imply that the individual can create personal meaning for himself independent of social considerations; that the mind can divest itself of its own emotional heritage; that an individual is capable of such a degree of dispassionate objectivity that he can look without flinching directly at those systems of belief that cover his naked insecurity—the sense of helplessness in which we are born, the sense of death toward which we are headed —and above all, that we can examine our own sexual drives and hungers, not to dismiss them but to channel them, subjecting them to conscious control.

Observe how this differs from Buddhist ideals of detachment. In that tradition drives are examined not to control them but to obliterate them, to make them inconsequential. To release oneself is not to continue to participate in the world but to withdraw from it and, indeed, to withdraw from any sense of self.

Psychoanalysis teaches us that we have been unduly rigidified; that we remain enslaved by the unresolved passions of childhood; that despite our ideal of autonomy we are still caught by destructive urges and sexual passions; that we have been traumatized and, in responding to trauma, find ourselves programmed by unconscious needs. The solution offered is to free ourselves by cutting the ties that bind us as children to our grossly imperfect parents. Family life for most of us is a bad karma from which we must seek deliverance. Indeed, we can seek deliverance by loosening our ties to the familial past, by seeking new meaning in the autonomous present. It is our responsibility to be in control of ourselves. But utilization of our "will power" is not sufficient without also discovering the roots of our incapacities in neurotic fixations. Only by dissolving these rigidifications can we control our behavior and adapt to reality in a more flexible manner. ("Reality" is rarely spelled out.)

Morita therapy seems directly concerned with forms of neurosis that are similarly caused by a problem of weakness of will. *Shinkeishitsu* occurs in those individuals who lack the will to mobilize their energy to perform what is expected of them by others as well as by themselves. They come to therapy not simply because they have symptoms such as shyness or fear of people (which are experienced by many Japanese) but because they are incapacitated in the performance of their daily occupations by such symptoms. And so, it is not surprising that the cure promised to them is not necessarily alleviation of internal symptoms but the capacity to function as expected in one's proper social role. There is no questioning of the ultimate values related to one's role. There is no questioning of the legitimacy of the alienation that one may quietly feel or of the doubts about what one is doing. Therapy is not undertaken to probe into the meaning that one has given to one's life. Rather, Morita therapy and the other quiet therapies reaffirm social purposes without question, whatever they may be in the particular.

This conforms to a long tradition in Zen Buddhism. The warrior that sought solace in Zen practice did so not to question his loyalty to his master or the rationality of the cause to which he was to dedicate his life. Rather, basic absurdity was assumed—the absurdity of all existence. The solution to malaise was to remove the observational ego's interference with the performance of one's particular destiny. That is, Zen practice was used to reduce the disruptive interference of doubt and self-consciousness, an interference that might have prevented the spontaneous execution of what was expected. Just as the trained Zen swordsman automatically responds to subtle stimuli, so the proper Japanese automatically performs his daily task despite the discordant inclinations of his individual self.

It is not through the development of a self-seeking introspection that one finds social healing, but through the removal of behavioral obstructions, the inner doubts and speculations that impede proper performance. It isn't that the Japanese seek to repress emotions. They seek to experience emotions without letting them interfere with behavior. Sensory pleasure is to be experienced. This is different from ruminating on it. Life is not a denial of feelings but a productive activity. Self-worth arises out of accomplishment, especially what is accomplished for others.

In Japan the "individual" will is defined as a part of selfish immaturity. The true individual finds his maturation in willing to be at one with the purposes of a social group. A woman loses herself in her family roles; a man's occupation may take him away from his family but he also finds familial-like social bonds and a sense of loyalty and dedication directed toward his occupational group. He symbolically takes his place somewhere within an age grading system: status and hierarchy are never overcome by a concept of universal brotherhood transcending differences of age. The Japanese in all their concepts of relationship can relate as peers only with those of the same symbolic age. There are bonds of friendship that work only for age mates; lifelong classmates who graduate at the same time are symbolically equal. Those who have gone before must remain elder brothers and sisters. Those who come after are little brothers and sisters. One never seeks for change in ultimate inequality. One cannot presume to do away with differentials of age, whether expressed toward parents and teachers or even toward an older sibling.

Therefore the Japanese, given this very basic premise in the ordering of human interaction, cannot follow a type of therapy that seeks to transcend age differences and remove a permanent status differential between parent and child. The child cannot dare to objectify or look dispassionately at the inadequacies of the parent who may have caused him to develop an unresolvable neurotic rigidification. How in Japan can one utilize therapeutically a theory that teaches that there is unavoidable destructiveness and jealousy directed toward parents, that there are sexual feelings bound up in our hatred of our parents, that maternal figures may not be all-loving but may indeed have been depriving or have caused us to develop poorly? Such concepts cannot be pursued by a Japanese who wishes to remain Japanese. Once such a Pandora's box of rage is opened, the quietness and harmony that are one's life goal can no longer be realized. There is no reconciliation with infantile and childish rage; it cannot be turned off again. The Japanese fear most profoundly the inability to deal with inchoate anger. It can only be viewed as leading to a final destructive oblivion.

What is sought instead is tranquility—forms of internal manipulation of thought that lead to quietude, not anger. Rather than facing head-on the anxieties that block us from experiencing our primal sense of destructiveness or sexual attachment, so that the dark unconscious powers within us are laid to rest or at least brought to heel by conscious control, the Japanese learn to exercise control over thoughts in a more hypnotic way. Rather than exploring the miasmic marshes of early memory, they reconstruct the past. Experiences of deprivation are superceded by illusions of past indulgence, of newly created, if not actually experienced, acts of kindness. One comes to reinterpret past behavior of parents as possible expressions of love, perhaps previously ignored or misinterpreted because of one's immature selfishness. The negative balance of one's own experience is counterweighed by Japanese belief in the innate goodness of all mothers. The cultural tradition of maternal sacrifice is available to those whose own fallible memories have led to experiences of resentment rather than gratitude; so one's experiences are gradually redefined to partake of those of the collectivity and there is a growing sense of having received love through sacrifice. Just as a Christian convert comes to believe in the love of Christ, Japanese deeply believe in their religion of the family.

It follows that any therapy seeking critically to examine family failure in Japan cannot be popular. Japanese religions, moreover, whether those of the past or the so-called new religions of the present, are likewise more effective when they redirect a sense of gratitude and obligation back toward parental figures. They cause the individual to reassess and reinterpret what his experiences have been, opening up a capacity for gratitude for favors received— even in those cases where patently the parent did not deliver. Parental figures become symbols and fictions, not actual people. The mother is romanticized as an all-giving person, and the image is reinforced in all forms of Japanese popular culture. This projection of benevolence is not limited to maternal figures. A father, to serve as an ideal, is best removed from daily contact. The actual individual does not then disrupt, by his imperfect presence, the needed illusion of continual benevolence. The authority figure in Japan is conceived of as a distant figure who bestows benevolence on those over whom he exercises power. This conception is as yet today a part of the image of the ideal father. It is the mother's role to maintain such an image of authority whether or not the occupant of the role in the family deserves that respect. In effect, there is a constant social reinforcement of belief in parental images.

Japanese ideas about child rearing traditionally are explicit concerning the effects of neglect and deprivation on a child. Takeo Doi, in his discussion of *The Anatomy of Dependency*, describes Japanese folk concepts of child rearing. *Hinikureta* (warping) is caused by the frustration of one's sense of dependency. For that reason Japanese mothers are encouraged to indulge their children in the early childhood period, to strengthen their sense of being

loved and cared for. Later negative attitudes toward social authority are directly linked in Japanese thought to earlier experiences of
maternal neglect. Again, the social atmosphere in Japan is condu-
cive to having the individual believe in an indulgent mother.*

The expectation of care—the payoff of being dependent—continues into adulthood for many Japanese. It colors the conception
of education and career choice. Youthful Japanese are quite prone
in their secondary socialization to become "imprinted" by some
mentor, or benevolent *sensei*—literally, an individual born before,
a predecessor, an individual who, forever a generation ahead in the
age grading system, bestows upon those who come after him the
key secrets of mastering a given art. The sensei very often is no
more real in actual experience than is the idealized parent. The
sensei as an idealized authority figure must be created if he does
not exist, to paraphase Voltaire. He is necessary as one toward
whom one can direct a continual flow of gratitude.

Many Japanese are ambivalent today. They wish to be rationally
motivated. They wish to be totally instrumental. They do not like
the fetters of social domination that seem to tie them together in an
inescapable network of mutual obligations. Yet they find their own
dependent needs are what binds them in this network and, if they
will admit it, they find such a system satisfying. Nurturance, the
sense of being bestowed upon, is still deeply sought. The individual,
whatever his hope for detachment and a capacity to function instrumentally in an autonomous way, is curiously prone to the blan-
dishments of hierarchy, subjecting himself to someone envisioned
as stronger and more capable. For a Japanese, strength does not
imply punishment or hostile domination: it still implies the possibility that someone will gratify one's deepest dependent needs.

We have discussed dependency and gratitude at great length.
One may ask, with impatience, what about the major concern in

---

*I sincerely doubt this belief can be strongly maintained on a collective basis in the
United States. It is far less likely that an American can draw on any such belief to
overcome his personal experience of resentment. In the contemporary American plu-
ralistic climate it is more likely that an individual sense of deprivation will be reinforced by transferring it to some social sense of deprivation experienced collectively
by an exploited class or ethnic group. Maternal deprivation is denied not by a reinterpretation of one's early experiences; rather, it is denied by refocusing one's deep
sense of resentment on an unjust, depriving society.

psychoanalysis—guilt? Where does guilt fit in? Is it true, as has often been stated, that Japanese are members of a shame culture and that Western concepts of guilt do not apply? In my volume *Socialization for Achievement*, I have argued strongly against the idea of Japan as a shame culture. In fact, I have contended that the Japanese in general are prone to guilt, that they are highly internalized, and that the nature of their internalization is the key to understanding the manifestly inherent need for achievement and social accomplishment which we witness in their economic as well as artistic endeavors.

Reynolds points out that

A failure on the part of an individual practicing therapy is not attributed to the therapy but to the failure of the individual to be able to follow the prescriptive regime. The locus of the problem is located not in the society or in its external relationship but within the person himself.

This is an important point to consider from the standpoint of the influence of the social atmosphere on the individual. Whereas an American delinquent is more apt to find social beliefs directing resentment outward toward the society in general, Japanese delinquents find themselves in a social atmosphere in which they are constrained toward developing a deeper capacity for internalization. To the majority of Japanese, authorities, including the police, are not automatically seen as oppressive. There is still a firm belief in the possibility of benevolence. The fact that historically the Japanese have developed extreme susceptibility to group pressures toward conformity, as a result of their tightly knit feudal organization, and the fact that Japanese are interdependent do not argue against their manifest capacity for achievement and potential for guilt should sacrificing parents not be repaid. The underlying need for such justification through accomplishment is the force that moves Japan in its massive transformation of essentially feudal social structures into perhaps the most efficient of today's modern industrial societies.

What about Japanese neurotic malaise? Are we not to find there also problems of guilt needing relief? I have argued that guilt is not to be considered simply as a fear of punishment. In fact, if one truly believes in a vengeful God, one is not guilty. One is simply afraid.

Guilt resides more in the human capacity to understand the feeling of pain in others as well as one's fearful capacity to produce it by one's own destructive behavior. There are three basic forms of discipline related to child rearing. The two we usually consider are punishment (physical punishment very often) and abandonment or separation. We neglect to consider the induction of guilt through sacrificial behavior on the part of a suffering parent.

Parental suffering can be tied to "bad behavior" which hurts the parent. The Japanese mother has perfected the technique of inducing guilt in her children by her quiet suffering. The child comes to regard certain unsanctioned social behavior as having consequences for one's parents as well as for oneself. The mother, assuming responsibility for the behavior of her children, is the one who suffers the consequences of their bad behavior. The child knows full well that should he behave in an unsocial way, should he be remiss as a member of his family, should he not strive to do well, he will bring sorrow and suffering to the person he loves. At the same time, he is progressively disciplined to take on onerous tasks, to submit himself to the difficult work of learning, to control his emotions so they will not be disruptive. Certainly, the type of discipline imposed upon the individual and the burdens he assumes are frustrating, and at times he must deeply wish to remove the sources of frustration. He has within himself the knowledge of these destructive capacities, but he is not able to release them without annihilating his objects of love and dependency as well as annihilating himself.

It is extremely difficult for Japanese to enter the recesses of their own unconscious to examine the negative feelings held toward parents. Parents are double images. As is true of parents elsewhere, they are the sources of conflict in early experience. But unlike situations in which religious representations have become separated from parental images, in Japan parents are at the same time the very religious idols which carry for Japanese the sign of ultimate personal security. In fact, the deepest sense of guilt is felt not for an offense against God as it is represented in Western thought. For a Japanese the deepest reservoir of guilt is not to return the sense of love and gratitude created by parents.

There is some difficulty in perceiving Japanese guilt theoretically, if not clinically, because psychoanalysis, the psychological system most often consulted by us for help in understanding the mechanisms involved in guilt, tends in itself to be strongly influenced by Western ethical values. In describing psychosexual development psychoanalytic writers tend to emphasize the "super ego" on the one hand, and the concepts of personal individuation and autonomy on the other. For the Westerner a major goal of maturation is freedom of the ego from irrational social control as well as from excessive internalized super ego demands. For an understanding of the Japanese this emphasis is somewhat out of focus. Maturational ideals of traditional Japanese society put far more emphasis on concepts of belonging and on adult role identity. And one must say that there is some truth in the Japanese point of view as well as in that fostered by Western thought.

Returning to concepts of naikan therapy or Morita therapy, we can see how they are taken very directly from major concerns in Japanese culture with gratitude and guilt. The self-reflections of a person in naikan therapy, for example, are supposed to help him find within himself how he has been resentful from an early age and therefore has harbored destructive feelings. He did not understand properly that the sources of his discomfort are to be found in his own behavior rather than in a parent's neglect, depreciation, or deprivation. He must evaluate his own feelings, his own egocentric demands, his own distortions of the past that blind him to the goodness of others. Reynolds, in his own experience of naikan therapy, found that it worked on him in this manner. At one point, he felt that "there were social debts to repay, feelings of gratitude to be expressed, and tasks to be carried out."

What occurs in naikan therapy overall is a reorganization of one's recollections. A framework is created for reordering the past. The past, in effect, is mythologized to release a capacity for gratitude. Christian conversion is a Western analogue. In Japan, however, repentance is not for love of Christ and his sacrifice but most often for love of mother and her sacrifice. There is a reversal of one's instrumentalization of relationships—of using others as tools for satisfying selfish needs. One turns rather toward an attitude of being able to give to others. There is a liberation of energy in finding in oneself a capacity for self-sacrifice comparable to that experienced from an all-loving being, whether this being is seen as a Christ figure or as a mother figure.

I hope these reflections may help bridge Western expectations of explanation and Reynolds' experiential observations. These comments, however, will not satisfy those who wish for some theoretical construction of the psychological principles that underlie the efficacy of the quiet therapies. Suffice it to say, in my psychological work in Japan I have not found the Japanese to be "different" psychologically. One can, if one so desires, attempt to explain shinkeishitsu in Western terms. The Japanese experiencing this malaise resemble their Western counterparts who, at the turn of the century, were labeled "psychesthenic" or "neurasthenic," and who today would perhaps be diagnosed as manifesting some form of obsessive compulsive neurosis. But so to classify them is to categorize them in Western terms. The Japanese experience of such malaise remains very Japanese in content.

If we were to use our Western terminology, we could say that Morita therapy can be presumed to work best with certain forms of obsessive compulsive neurosis, that it also works with individuals given to certain phobic concerns of the obsessional nature. These symptoms can be very debilitating for some. They can prevent the individual from working, but under a supportive form of therapy the symptoms can be sufficiently alleviated to allow the individual to return productively to his occupation. The individual learns to live with his inner malaise. He is not necessarily "cured" by its removal.

One of the reasons we might be concerned with knowing or understanding these therapies in Western terms is the pragmatic possibility of applying them to Western subjects. Would such regimes of therapy work in the United States? I have already commented on such a possibility. Seen cross-culturally, they could work only if a sufficient social climate of belief and implicit support allows the individual to gain for himself a sense of participating in an efficacious procedure. Like religious conversion, therapeutic help depends somewhat on the exercise of faith. But whereas the content of belief in the first instance remains directly religious, a modern mode of secular thought is dominant in the second, and faith is in the healer and his method of therapy.

Freud and some of his more dispassionate followers have not been too sanguine about the widespread applicability of psychoanalysis as the therapy of choice for most psychological difficulties. Hence one must consider other forms of healing that depend on faith in the healer and his remedy. A willingness to endure the rigors of a therapeutic procedure in good faith is the first step toward a better command over one's internal difficulties. Practice of a quiet therapy can work. Let us hope that our social climate continues to support the value of the individual in secular as well as religious thought. To this extent it shall support the human hope that one can "overcome" on an individual as well as a collective level, whatever the negative karma passed on to us.

GEORGE DE VOS

University of California, Berkeley

References

Bando, Shojun. Jodo Buddhism in the light of Zen. *Buddhist Japan: introductory essays on Japanese Buddhism.* Tokyo: Buddhist Laymen's Association, 1962.

Csikszentmihalyi, Mihaly. *Beyond boredom and anxiety.* San Francisco: Jossey-Bass, 1976.

Dumoulin, Heinrich, S. J. *A history of Zen Buddhism.* Boston: Beacon, 1969.

Frankl, Viktor E. *Man's search for meaning.* New York: Washington Square Press, 1963.

Furlong, William B. The fun in fun. *Psychology Today,* June 1976, pp. 35–38, 80.

Grossberg, John M. Brain wave feedback experiments and the concept of mental mechanisms. *Behavior Therapy and Experimental Psychiatry,* 1972, *3*:245–251.

Herrigel, Eugen. *Zen in the art of archery.* New York: Random House, 1971.

Hirai, Tomio. *Zen meditation therapy.* Tokyo: Japan Publications, 1975.

Hiresaki, Tetsu. *Kokoro no byoki* [Sickness of the heart]. 2 vols. Tokyo: Furinshobo, 1968.

———. Shadan ryoho [Shadan therapy]. *Seishin Ryoho Kenkyu,* 1972, *3*:1–9.

Ishida, Rokuro. Naikan analysis. *Psychologia,* 1969, *12*:81–92.

Iwai, Hiroshi, and Reynolds, David K. Morita therapy: The views from the West. *American Journal of Psychiatry,* 1970, *126*(7):1031–1036.

Kaketa, K., Sugita, T., and Akitani, T. Iwayura shadan ryoho ni yoru chiryo kekka no kensa [A study of the results of shadan therapy]. *Seishin Ryoho Kenkyu,* 1972, *3*:20–31.

Kapleau, Philip. *The three pillars of Zen.* Boston: Beacon, 1965.

Kitsuse, John I. Moral treatment and reformation of inmates in Japanese prisons. Paper read at the First International Congress for Social Psychiatry, 1964. Reprinted in *Psychologia*, 1965, 8:9–23.

———. A method of reform in Japanese prisons. In Schneps, Maurice, and Coox, Alvin D., eds. *The Japanese Image*, 1966, 2:1–7.

Kodani, Hirumi. Shinkeishitsu no hontai to sono ryoho [The basic character of neurosis and its cure]. *Naikan*, 1969, 3:32–50.

Koga, Yoshiyuki. On Morita therapy. *Jikeikai Medical Journal*, 1967, 14:73–99.

Kora, T. and Ohara, K. Morita therapy. *Psychology Today*, October 1973, pp. 63–68.

Murase, Takao, and Johnson, Frank. Naikan, Morita and Western psychotherapy: A comparison. Paper read at the American Psychiatric Association Meeting, 1973.

Murase, Takao, and Reynolds, David. Naikan therapy. Nara: Naikan Training Center, n.d.

Naikan Training Center. Naikan information sheet. Mimeographed, n.d.

Ohara, Kenshiro, and Reynolds, David. Morita psychotherapy: Characteristics of a Japanese treatment for neurosis. Unpublished manuscript, n.d.

Reynolds, David K. Directed behavior change: Japanese psychotherapy in a private mental hospital. Unpublished doctoral dissertation. University of California at Los Angeles, 1969.

———. *Morita psychotherapy*. Berkeley: University of California Press, 1976.

———, and Kiefer, Christie W. Cultural adaptability as an attribute of therapies. *Culture, Medicine, and Psychiatry*, 1977, 1:395–412.

———, and Moacanin, Radmila. Eastern therapy: Western patient. *Japanese Journal of Psychotherapy Research*, 1977, 3(2).

———, and Yamamoto, Joe. Morita psychotherapy in Japan. *Current Psychiatric Therapies*, 1973, 13:219–227.

Sato, Koji. *Shinri Zen* [Psychological Zen]. Osaka: Sogensha, 1961.

———, ed. *Zenteki ryoho, naikan ho* [Zenlike therapy and naikan]. Tokyo: Bunkodo, 1972.

Sato, Wakio. Shigeki shadan ryoho ni yoru chiryo keiken [Experience in treatment by means of stimulus deprivation therapy]. *Seishin Ryoho Kenkyu*, 1972, 3:10–19.

Smith, Adam. The benefits of boredom. *Psychology Today*, April 1976, pp. 46–51.

Stryk, Lucien, and Ikemoto, Takashi, eds. *Zen: Poems, prayers, sermons, anecdotes, interviews*. New York: Doubleday Anchor Books, 1965.

Suedfeld, Peter. The benefits of boredom. *American Scientist*, 1975, 63(1):60–69.

Suzuki, Daisetz T. *Zen and Japanese culture.* New York: Random House, 1959.

Suzuki, D. T. et al. *Zen Buddhism and psychoanalysis.* New York: Grove Press, 1963.

Suzuki, Tomonori, and Suzuki, Ryu. A follow-up of neurotics treated by Morita therapy. Paper presented at the 6th World Congress of Psychiatry. Honolulu, 1977.

Takeuchi, Katashi. On "naikan" method. *Psychologia,* 1965, 8:2–8.

Wienpahl, Paul. *Zen diary.* New York: Harper & Row, 1970.

Yamamoto, Haruo et al. *Naikan ryoho* [Naikan therapy]. Tokyo: Igaku Shoin, 1972.

Yokoyama, Keigo. *Seiza ryoho* [Seiza therapy]. Osaka: Sogensha, 1974.

Yoshimoto, Ishin, ed. *Kurushimi no kaiketsuho* [Method for relief from suffering]. Nara: Naikan Training Center, 1971.

_____. *Naikanho-he no go-annai* [A guide to naikan]. Nara: Naikan Training Center, 1973.

Production Notes

This book was typeset on
the Unified Composing System by
The University Press of Hawaii

The text typeface is
Compugraphic Caledonia and the display
typeface is Benguiat.

Offset presswork and binding were
done by Halliday Lithograph. Text paper is
Glatfelter P & S Offset, basis 55.